Man from Mono

Lily Mathieu La Braque

A memoir of the La Braque family of Mono Basin as told by George La Braque, Sr. to his daughter Lily.

NEVADA ACADEMIC PRESS
P.O. Box 60134
Reno, Nevada 89506

Published by Nevada Academic Press, which
specializes in regional publishing projects.

Library of Congress Catalog Card Number 84-90591
Hard Cover ISBN 0-9613730-0-8
Paperback ISBN 0-9613730-1-6
Printed in the United States of America

As soon as I got over the pass the wind was blowing terrifically. I looked at my beloved Mono Lake, a vision of scenic grandeur that occurs no place else in the world, and there to the east rose the dust, and it was rising to a height of over 10,000 feet.

Enid Larson describing the view
from Tioga Pass on June 28, 1976

"Storm Over Mono Lake": photographer Larry Ford caught this dramatic view of Mono Lake as winds blew 60 miles per hour.

Table of Contents

To Betty La Braque,
Wife — Mother

Family
(Excerpts from a poem by Stevenson Higa)

...It is the *strength of family* that protects in the time
of great conflict.

...It is the *togetherness of family* that lends the strong arm of support
in tme of weakness.

...It is the *comfort of family* that heals
in time of grief.

...It is the *love of family* that beautifies
our precious moments of life.

...It is the *unity of family* that eternally seeks the infinite power
of the heaven here on earth.

And what is life when there is no family?

It is the dry, parched soil of a heartless desert...

Illustration Credits

Photographs not listed here are from the La Braque family archives. Maps are by Lily Mathieu La Braque and Emily Hart.

Front Cover: Jim Stroup
Back Cover: Gerald Yongue
Page v: Larry Ford

Chapter	Page	*Courtesy of...*
1	7	Demmitt Felesena
1	10	Frasher Studios
1	12	(Top) — Frasher Studios
1	12	(Bottom) — Katy Bell
2	14–15	Dorothy Hathway
2	16	Donald Rambeau, *Carson Valley News*
2	18	Wallis McPherson
3	21	Frasher Studios
3	23	(Top and Center) — Leo Mattly
3	23	(Bottom) — Tom Buckly
3	27	(Left) — James Keller
3	27	(Right) — August Hess
3	29	Elaine Bell
3	31	Ruth Lewis
6	45	Elaine Bell
6	46	Alice Dolan
7	50	(Top) — Katy Bell
7	50	(Bottom left) — John Lundy
7	50	(Bottom right) — Katy Bell
7	51	Katy Bell
7	52	(Left) — Katy Bell
7	52	(Right) — Elaine Bell
7	54	Lily Mathieu La Braque
7	55	Dorothy Andrews
7	56	Jerry Andrews
8	59	The late Lee Symmonds
8	60	(Right) — Dorothy Andrews

Foreword

Man from Mono originated from many wonderful stories told to our family by my father, George La Braque, who was born near the shores of Mono Lake on May 3, 1899.

The stories were told randomly over a period of many years. I've written them, as much as possible, in my father's words and in his perspective, and set them within a framework in order to give a rounded picture of how early "Basinites" lived, how they reveled in idyllic summers, and coped with frigid winters. I've tried to lend perspective and atmosphere to my family's beginnings at Mono Lake, covering the period 1885–1935.

You will learn about several tragedies and triumphs of my relatives, early Mono Basin settlers: the Filosenas from Italy and the La Braques from the Pyrenees in France.

The old ways and hazardous times have faded away— but not so long ago, when you come right down to it.

Nobody writes a book entirely by herself; and to the many people who have patiently answered my questions, shared their memories and their photographs, and encouraged me each step of the way, I owe a great deal of gratitude.

Special thanks go to my publisher, Shelly Lescott of Nevada Academic Press, for her unwavering support, to Demila Jenner, for assisting me with her literary expertise and for her faith in this project, Marion Maize, the designer, as well as Native American artist Raymond Andrews and David Gaines of the Mono Lake Committee. My gratitude also goes to Bill Banta, Mrs. Pearl Mattly, Katy Bell, Jim Keller, Bob Bell, Tom Buckley, Alice Dolan and Dan Bryant.

Thanks a million to all of you.

Lily Mathieu La Braque
Lee Vining
June 1984

Jerome Bardanare La Braque.

Chapter 1

Death and Vengeance

"I'll get him for this!" threatened Jerome as he left his home in France to come to America.

My father, Jerome Bardanare La Braque, was born on his parents' sheep ranch on January 4, 1861, in the shadow of the Pyrenees at Basses, France. When he was 17, he left home, arriving in America with a single purpose in mind — to track down and kill the man who had killed his father.

Family legend links Jerome with Jerome Napoleon, brother of Bonaparte but frankly the details are sketchy.

He was a small man, as were the Napoleons, standing 5'7" and weighing 165 pounds. He had a sister Marie, who became a nun, and a brother Joseph. Their mother, of small stature also, weighed less than a hundred pounds. Carlos, their father, stood over six feet. He was a big hunk of a man.

Tragedy struck one misty day as Carlos exchanged harsh words with a debtor. As they argued, Carlos made a threatening move toward the man, who happened to be holding an umbrella.

The man thrust the umbrella toward Carlos, who threw up his arm to deflect the weapon. The point pierced Carlos' eye. He died within the hour.

His relatives and friends mourned his loss and heatedly discussed plans to deal with the assailant; but before they could act he left the country. More than a year had gone by when word reached the family that letters from the murderer had been received, postmarked, "San Francisco."

The killing had not been forgotten and it was felt that the man should be dealt with. A collection was raised for passage and expenses, and young Jerome was chosen to settle the score. Leaving Joseph in charge of the La Braque affairs, Jerome sailed for New York, working on the ship to make extra money. Upon arriving, he continued by train for San Francisco.

Jerome spoke only French, so he went directly to a French hotel where the Basques congregated. He got a job as a herder some miles from the city. Before long, his new friends shortened his name to "J.B." — it clung to him throughout his life.

J.B. persisted, doggedly tracking his father's killer. After many inquiries he learned that the man had been seen in a restaurant the previous week. Nervously, he began closing in. Somehow, the killer had found out that Jerome was looking for him and headed for Bakersfield, with J.B. following close behind. J.B. went to work there as a sheepherder, passing first through Mono Basin. All the while, he continued his search.

One day, as J.B. tended his flock, he saw a man coming over the crest of a hill. He shivered in recognition. His heart leaped to his throat, as he stood face to face with his father's murderer.

J.B. had equipped himself for this eventuality. He quickly drew a large .44 pistol which he kept under his belt.

"I have a score to settle with you," he said, steadily leveling the gun at the man, who made no move to run or defend himself.

The man shouted, "Go ahead — shoot!! Your father's death was an accident! If he hadn't thrown his arm up, the umbrella wouldn't have pierced his eye. I haven't had a good night's sleep since. I can't get the picture out of my mind." He added, "I'd be better off dead."

J.B.'s thirst for vengeance lessened as he realized the logic of what the man was saying. J.B. saw the man was truly sorry for that far-away accident. He slowly lowered the gun and returned it to its hiding place.

There was nothing more to say.

The man turned slowly and went back over the hill to his flock.

J.B. kept thinking about the poor wretched man, and he wondered what his family and friends were going to say when they found out about the strange turn of events.

Early the next morning, J.B. walked over the hill to tell the man to forget the incident, and to wish him well; but the man was nowhere to be seen.

Instead, a new herder told him that the man had left hurriedly for parts unknown. He was never heard of again.

The Immigrants

In Italy, southeast of where Jerome's story begins, the Filosena family was flourishing. Their sons and daughters would soon be leaving for

America. In the Alpine-like setting of Mono Basin, the La Braque and Filosens would eventually be joined together.

The earliest and principal Etruscan center in northern Italy was the place the Romans later called Bonionia (the modern Bologna); the Etruscans knew it as Felsina. This province overlooked the River Reno (Rhenus). The Filosens are remembered for their remarkable bronze works. Many unearthed in recent years are pictures in *The Etruscans.*[1]

The name "Filosena" is derived from "Filosen," and was the name used as the clan moved farther north.

In more recent times, 1845 to be exact, the Filosena clan turns up in the province of Lombardo. In the town of Giosotto, on the border of Austria and Italy, and not far from Milan, Giorgio Lester Filosena was born.

As a man, Giorgio raised vineyards and numerous children. Seven of them came to America: George Martin, Peter, Dominico, Angelo, Joseph, Carlos, and a daughter Rachael.

From what I can gather, George Martin was the first to arrive in New York in 1870. He went to Illinois, worked in the coal mines, and later settled in St. Anne, Illinois, where many of his descendents still reside.

Carlos, the family rogue, earned his passage money by the light of the Alpine moon, smuggling heavy packs of salt and tobacco across border trails to Switzerland. Several times he was nearly captured by the border patrol which was, fortunately, one jump behind.

Carlos continued his perilous treks for two years, somehow eluding his would-be captors. Often, he had to hide for many hours before continuing on the narrow trail. As soon as he had enough saved for his ticket to America he was on his way to join George Martin in the Illinois mines.

The lure of California gold beckoned Carlos westward. Mailing his passport home for brother Joseph to use (the brothers were all look-alikes), he drifted south into Texas. He was a cowboy when he came into Nevada on a cattle drive, having signed on as a herd driver.

At Genoa, Nevada's oldest town, Carlos was eventually joined by brothers Dominico, Angelo, and later, Joseph. There they became woodcutters in the pine nut area high in the hills of eastern Douglas County. It was 1875.

Evidently there was some dissension among the woodcutters, because in May, a man named Giovanni Imperali came down from the hills, reporting to authorities that several months earlier, Dominico had been seen wielding an ax against his own brother.

---

[1] *The Etruscans* — Michael Grant, Charles Scribner & Sons, New York, 1980.

The incident received extensive news coverage by the *Carson Valley News*[2] and the *Territorial Enterprise* of Virginia City. It was called a "Cain and Abel" drama.

Under suspicion for murder, Dominico fled to Italy, where he was chased about and finally captured by the police as he loudly proclaimed his innocence. King Emanuel II commissioned Secretary of State Hamilton Fish to ferret out the truth.

The Imperalis were found to be cousins of the Filosenas, and the families were jealous of each other. Furthermore, there were only vague and unauthenticated reports about the alleged murder, and no corpse had ever been found. The case was dismissed. Justice may or may not have been served, but the close ties of immigrants to their homeland cannot be disputed.

Dominico remained in Italy; Angelo went to San Francisco; and Carlos and Joseph continued their woodcutting at Genoa, Nevada, selling all they could cut for four dollars a cord.

Tents were the only housing available, and the brothers, tough though they were, suffered severe hardships for two winters in the sub-zero temperatures. Then they pulled out.

Carlos (who boasted that until he was 13, he had never worn a pair of shoes) and Joseph headed for Mono Basin and on east to Mono Mills, where a cookshack and bunkhouse were offered to workers who cut logs for the mines of the nearby boomtown of Bodie.

Later, the brothers went to work as hardrock miners themselves at the May Lundy mine. This mine, located directly behind Lundy Lake at an elevation over 9000 feet, could only be reached by a steep, winding road in summer and on foot or skis in winter.

"Charlie" and "Joe," as the brothers had been re-named by their mining buddies, were dubbed, "ninety day wonders," or "greenhorns." Mono Basin reminded Charlie of the Alps, and he saved his earnings toward the day when he could acquire a plot of land and send for the rest of the family. As a matter of fact, along with two partners, he eventually homesteaded one hundred and sixty acres overlooking Mono Lake. After some haggling, they divided this land into parcels. Charlie's share was to the north, and had very good water rights. Later, for convenience, he would build his ranch house near the creek which ran through the property.

One of the partners eventually sold his property to Louis De

---

[2] *Carson Valley News,* May 8, 1875.

Mary Filosena, Agnes, and Peter, taken at Ellis Island, New York.

Chambeau, the other to Albert Silvester. Albert, who built a large two-story home with a fine orchard, served as deputy sheriff.

Charlie sent for his wife, Mary (Possi), and their two small children, Agnes and Peter. Arriving in New York in 1885, Mary was terrified. She spoke only a few words of English, and she was detained at Ellis Island for over two weeks. Her passport had listed two *male* children.

She carried with her a letter from Charlie instructing her how to board the train for Nevada; and with kind people helping her, in due time the family arrived in Carson City, where Charlie was waiting impatiently. They visited relatives and rested for a few days, then took the stage to Bridgeport, California, continuing to Mono Lake by wagon. As they came out of Cottonwood Canyon, Charlie pulled the team up to rest and give Mary her first view of Mono Lake.

Mary was thrilled by its beauty, and as time passed she grew to love her new home. It was good that she did, for although her heart sought its way back to the Alps many times, Mary never again returned to her homeland. She spent the rest of her life on the ranch, working in the fields, peddling vegetables and dairy products and raising her family. Including me, years later.

Grandmother Mary and son George in front of their new ranch house.

My grandmother Mary, who died in 1931, is buried on the hill overlooking Mono Lake. Three of her children were laid to rest near her: Mary and Peter, who had made the first crossing with her, and my dear Uncle George, crippled and hunchbacked.

The Filosenas and La Braques of Mono Lake

When the Filosenas were first reunited on the ranch, they lived in a small one-room cabin while Charlie constructed their new ranch house. It had two stories, with two bedrooms upstairs. Downstairs there was a parlor, three bedrooms, and a milk room where the milk was covered to cool and the cream skimmed off. Connected to the house was a large garage where the carriage and firewood were kept, together with a large, foot-peddled, stone knife sharpener.

A large cellar with a wooden door was out in front. Mary used this to store root vegetables, orchard fruit, and the many jars of preserves that she put up to tide her family over the frosty winters. The real mainstay of winter were the two wooden wine barrels that held either pork or beef, all raised on the ranch. They were preserved in salt brine and weighted down with a rock. The water had to be changed about once a month. My Uncle George and I had this task.

On Sundays, neighbors came from far and wide to watch Charlie's progress. The house was considered very grand. When it was finished it was painted a gleaming white.

Although more than a hundred years have passed, the ranch feebly stands in weatherbeaten shades of gold and brown. The large tree that I shinnied up so many times still guards the front door, and each Spring the old orchard in back valiantly displays a smattering of cherry, pear, and apple blossoms.

Charlie was very stubborn, and Mary — actually a kind-hearted woman — had a fierce temper which she exercised frequently in Charlie's direction. Their separation had not strengthened their relationship, and after a few stormy years Charlie moved to Nevada, where he found work on the railroad section at Lakeview, just outside of Carson City. He was a powerhouse of a man, *running* to work three miles and back, summer and winter.

On one of his visits to see George Martin in Illinois, Charlie, now divorced, met and married another "Mary" and fathered three more sons: Charlie, another Peter, and Lester.

Carlos and "Illinois" Mary with sons. (L. to r.: Pete, Charles, and Lester.)

Joseph Filosena.

My grandmother Mary was having quite a time of it, raising her family and running the ranch by herself. One day a big, strong fellow stopped by the creek to get a drink of water from the big metal dipper Mary kept there for passersby. He told her his name was Pete Roberts. She learned that he was looking for work. Mary made him an offer, promising him shares of the harvests for his salary. Roberts accepted.

In this way, Mary was able to continue peddling the produce and dairy products to the miners of Lundy and Jordan.

Charlie's brother Joe was still working at the May Lundy mine. He often visited at the ranch. After a time, Joe and Mary fell in love and got married. They had two children: Mary, who was born in 1889, and George, born in 1891.

One day, Joe had some trouble over a fur trade with the Paiute chief, One-eyed Jack, and two of his braves. Still furious about whatever it was that caused the dispute, Joe got into a fracas during a poker game at Lundy with some miners a few nights later.

The foreman of the mine came to the ranch the next day to discuss the incident. No one ever knew the details or what money was involved; but Joe was very worried.

Making some excuses, Joe kept to the house the next morning while the rest of the family went out to the fields. When they returned he was not to be seen. At first they thought nothing of it, assuming he had felt better and gone up to Lundy. But when Joe hadn't returned by evening, a thorough search was made. He was discovered in the blacksmith shop, about 75 feet from the garage. Dead. Hanging. Joe had hung himself.

Family and friends found it hard to believe. Joe had been a calm and quiet man. Mary was inconsolable and lamented his death for many years.

Joe was laid to rest in 1906, at the little hillside cemetery overlooking Mono Lake, where Mary later joined him. Fortunately, Pete Roberts continued to help with the ranch.

This was the Filosena family of Mono Lake, when young J.B. La Braque returned to Mono Basin and met dark-skinned, high-spirited Agnes Filosena, who had come over from Italy with mother Mary.

On J.B.'s trek to Bakersfield, hunting for his father's killer, he had become entranced by the rugged beauty of Mono Basin. Its lofty peaks, rugged terrain, and azure lake reminded him of his homeland in the Pyrenees. With this in mind, he bought his own flock of sheep; and in the spring of 1891, he brought them up the "long trail," through Mojave Desert. J.B. herded his sheep on foot, a distance of three hundred miles. Three good sheep dogs and two donkeys carrying provisions (salami, cheese, coffee, wine, bacon and pipe tobacco) were also along. The trail started at Bakersfield and ended when the sheep reached the summer range in the hills around Bodie.

At certain times of the year, J.B. grazed his sheep in pastures near the Filosena ranch.

A heady courtship which J.B. pursued with the beautiful, thirteen-year-old Agnes culminated in their marriage at Lundy on Christmas Day, 1895, thereby uniting the Filosena and La Braque families.

The Filosenas and La Braques established permanent roots in Mono Basin, along with neighbors of many other nationalities, colors, and creeds. Most had been drawn West by the lure of Bodie gold. They were warm-hearted, rough and ready pioneers, who gave flavor and variety to the land they shared with the local Paiute Indians.

Mono Basin was shaped by these peoples, with their deep beliefs and traditional values. Many pursued their former occupations. They cut forests, worked the mines, made laws, built schools and churches. And there were gamblers, lawmen, storekeepers, farmers, herders, black-smiths, stage drivers, doctors, writers, teachers, preachers and a good percentage of drifters and low-life as well.

Soon after their wedding, J.B. and Agnes bought a small parcel of land from Mary, which they homesteaded. It was a quarter of a mile north of the main ranch house.

J.B. built a small, two-room house with a cellar for them to live in. I was born there on May 3, 1899.

J.B. was a tough man, full of endurance and strength. He had a very bad temper, and when he was angry he was a good man to stay away from.

Singlehanded, using only a grub hoe and shovel, J.B. dug a ditch a quarter of a mile long to bring water to his homestead from Mill Creek. After clearing out the sagebrush, he put 60 acres into cultivation. The ground was fertile and the vegetables he and Agnes harvested were

Grazing near the ranch.

peddled readily at Lundy and Jordan. At times J.B. drove the mail stage from Mono Lake to Bodie.

Before long, J.B. had become a heavy gambler. He'd play for money or just for fun, and he always carried a deck of cards with him. When alone, he played solitaire.

In those days, "stud poker" was the popular game, and whenever there was a big game going on, J.B. made sure to be near at hand. When he had won big, he would come home with a wagonful of provisions and other goods, and we were all happy. Sometimes, he sold the produce and gambled away the money. He'd come home with his wagon and pockets empty, and my mother would cry.

A gambler's family, I learned, has to share the ups and downs of the gambler's life.

Once J.B. was gone for over a week, and my mother took turns being both furious and worried about him. She figured rightly that he was on one of his gambling sprees. Seeing one of his friends pass by on horseback, she called, "Have you seen Jerome?"

The man answered, "There's been a big game over at Bodie. J.B.'s behind me . . . he'll be here soon."

My mother thought of a scheme then and there to get even. She took her broom in one hand; with the other, she herded me down to the swamp where willows grew thickly along the path where J.B. would pass.

Soon Agnes saw a horse walking slowly in the distance. She recognized my father slouched way down, with his hat pulled over his ears. He was dozing. As he came alongside, Agnes dashed out of hiding, wildly waving her broom and sharply whacking the horse's forelegs. The startled animal whinnied and reared madly.

My father had won big. His hat and pockets were filled with money. Gold and silver coins flew through the air in a glittering shower. Some fell into the swamp, others into the sagebrush and along the path. As the horse reared, the saddle hitch broke, and J.B. took a nasty spill. My mother dropped her broom and all three of us scrambled to recover the coins, with J.B. contributing a loud and generous amount of French.

As time passed, every now and then a stray coin would turn up along the path. I often wonder how many we missed.

This dirt road north of Hammond's became part of Highway 395.

Jerome, standing by a Simplex Locomobile, in front of Hammond's.

Chapter 2

Lady Luck

J.B. was about to get lucky. You might say that that a murder was indirectly responsible.

Two miners, Jack and Dick Hammond, had come into Basin from the Sheepherder mine at Tioga. They were brothers, and they started a sawmill and toll gate operation at Lundy Canyon. One morning, as Dick stepped out behind his cabin, he was shot and killed. The motive wasn't known and the killer was never caught.

Jack sold his holdings and bought a store at Mono Lake from Tom Moyle, renaming it Hammond's Station.[1] He operated a stage stop and toll gate from the station, which sported a large hitching post out front. Hammond's Station quickly became the hub and buying center of Mono Basin.

In those days little money changed hands. Bartering was the usual method of exchange. Most of grandmother Mary's transactions were made at Hammond's, as you can see from the old ledger pages that follow.

The main attraction was Jack Hammond's telephone. It was one of the few in the Basin. On weekends folks relaxed, visited, and got news from outlying communities at Hammond's Station. And there were other attractions.

On Sunday afternoons it was not uncommon to see many Indian women and braves squatting on the front porch wearing colored shawls and blankets over their shoulders. The women wore red bandanas over their hair. The Indians played or wagered on the Hand Game. The Paiute Hand Game is similar to dice. It is played with sticks and two small "bones."

Inside Hammond's was a saloon, complete with card tables. The high proof "red-eye" served there was said to make the imbibers see double and feel single. Many times there were big stud poker games, too.

---

[1] It later was renamed Tioga Lodge.

J. P. HAMMOND

General Merchandise

ACCOUNT NO._____

Mono Lake, Cal._____ 190 9

SOLD TO *Mrs. Filoena*

Dec.	15	20 5 Joints Stove Pipe		1 75	
"	"	1 " Terra Cotta 1⁵⁵ Nails ¹⁰		1 60	3 35
Mar.	16	" 1 Sk. Salt "1 25 " returned 1 50			
		" 1 box Macaroni ⁹⁰		2 15	
April	20	" 1 pr. Shoes ³⁵⁰ Cinnamon ³⁰		3 80	
	"	" Envelopes		25	
May.	25	" 13¼ lbs Bacon ³⁹⁵		3 95	
	"	" 1 Lamp Chimney ¹⁵ 1 pr. Overalls ¹⁰⁶		1 15	
June	7	" 2¼ lbs. Cheese ⁵⁵ 13 lbs Bacon ³⁹⁶		4 45	13 60
	21	" 6¾ lbs. Bacon ²⁰⁰ 2 " Coffee ⁷⁰		2 70	16 30
July.	11	" 1 box Sections		1 25	
	13	" 1 " Guards ¹⁰⁰ Oil Can ³⁰		1 30	
	"	" 1 gal Machine Oil ¹⁵⁰ 1 box Shells ⁷⁵		2 25	
	21	" 11½ lbs Ham ³⁶⁵ 1 pr. Overalls ⁸⁵		4 50	
	28	" 8 lbs Bacon		2 72	
aug	4	" 6¾ lbs Bacon ²¹⁵ Writing Paper ⁴⁰		2 55	
	18	" 6¼ " " 2 00 Coffee ¹⁰⁰		3 00	
Sept	19	" 6 " " 1 92 1 Sk Salt 25		2 17	
	22	" 5 lbs Staples ⁵⁰ Twine ¹⁵ 1 pr. Shoes 4 25		4 90	
	27	" 7 " Bacon 2 24		2 24	26 68
Oct.	14	" 7 " " 4 can Sausage 1 50 4 pr Socks ³⁰		3 74	
	20	" 1 Empty Wine Barrell ⁷⁵ 1 pr. Overalls ¹⁰⁰		1 75	
	"	" Candles		50	5 99
	25	" 4 can Sausage ¹⁰⁰ 1 lb Coffee ³⁵		1 35	
	"	" Tobacco ⁶⁰ 5 Sf Flour 1 25		1 85	13 20
1911 April	20	" coffee 4 50 Salt 50 stock salt 1 25		6 25	
	"	" raisins 2 00 Box Macaroni 50 rice ¹⁰⁰		3 50	
	"	" corn meal ⁷⁵ barley 5 00 brush 50		6 25	
	"	" box cartridges		30	
1912 Jan	26	By amount carried forward		16 30	16 30
				1 63 6	1 6 30

Jack had recently purchased the Nay ranch from Cordelia Nay, who was unable to continue cultivation of the homestead after her husband, Winslow, drowned in Mono Lake.

Lady Luck smiled upon J.B. one evening in 1902, as he engaged in his favorite sport, gambling at Hammond's Saloon.

As he was preparing to return home with his supplies, Jack called out to him, "J.B., don't leave yet, we're going to have a big game."

"I'm already late," J.B. called out. "I better go on." Jack insisted,

ACCOUNT No. *6*			NAME *Mrs. Filosena*			TERMS
						RATING
SHEET No.			ADDRESS			LIMIT

Date	Items	Folio	V	Debits	Date	Items	Folio	V	Credits
Oct: 15	*To Mdse*			*76 65*	*June 25*	*By Cash*			*6 50*
					July 1	*" "*			*60*
					2	*" Vegetables*			*3 00*
					Aug. 5	*" 220 lbs. Pot.*			*8 80.*
					13	*" Vegetable*			*17 45*
					17	*" "*			*14 68*
					20	*" " 211 lb.*			*8 44*
					"	*" Sk Onions*			*3.0*
					"	*" " Vegetable*			*7 62*
					Sept: 22	*" Carrots*			*50*
						To Balance			*2 18*
				76 65					*76 65*
Oct. 18	*To Balance*			*2 18*	*18*	*By 299 lb. Beans*			*17 94*
	" Mdse			*32 20*	*22 " 27 " "*				*16 44*
				34 38					*34 38*
Jan 4	*To Mdse*			*3 35*	*Jan 4*	*By Cash*			*1 85*
Mar 16	*" "*			*2 15*	*" " Mdse. Returns*				*1 50*
					Mar 21	*" Cash*			*2 15*
				5 50					*5 50*
July 1	*To Mdse*			*16 30*	*Aug. 4*	*By Lettuce*			*50*
Oct: 1	*" "*			*26 68*	*Oct: 4*	*" 420 lbs. Beans 6+*			*25 20*
20	*" "*			*5 99*	*14 " 288 " " 6*				*17 28*
31	*" "*			*13 20*	*20 " 121 " Vegetable 54*				*3 63*
					Nov 1 To Balance				*1 55*
				62 17					*62 17*
1911									
Nov. 1	*To Balance*			*1 55*	*Nov. 12*	*By Cash*			*1 55*
1912									
Apr. 20	*To Mdse*			*1 6.30*	*Jan 26*	*By a/c transferred*			*1 6.30*

though, and J.B. threw caution to the winds as he retied his horse and went back inside.

There were four in the game besides Jack and J.B. It continued for two long days and nights, and J.B. was having a lucky streak. The four other men went broke, leaving only J.B. and Jack.

J.B. opened with three Queens. Jack matched the bet with the last of his cash.

Then J.B. drew cards and made a large raise. It was so quiet you

Nevada Day — Carson City. Minnie Turner tries her luck at Hand Game, while Carrie Bethyl (right) *and Tusuba* (left) *look on.*

could hear a pin drop. In one last, desperate effort to recoup his losses, Jack recklessly wagered the deed of the Nay ranch. The spectators pressed close. Jack was holding a full house, but this time, Lady Luck was smiling upon J.B.: he won with four Lucky Ladies!

Defeated, disappointed, and exhausted, Jack leaned over the table and fell into a deep sleep.

J.B. scooped up the cash and the deed, and was off, hardly believing his good fortune. He ran his high-spirited horse all the way home, arriving as the first rays of sun peeked through.

J.B. dismounted at a run, waking us as he shouted the glad news. Agnes was dubious until J.B. convinced her that the property was legally theirs. Jack, after all, had only recently come into its possession after Winslow Nay drowned in Mono Lake.

Misfortune on Mono

In 1896, Winslow and Cordelia Nay left Nevada's Carson Valley with their five children to homestead on the south shore of Mono Lake (about two miles south of Hammond's Station). The children attended the Mono Lake school, and the eldest son, Orville, later became a teacher. Winslow Nay became a county Supervisor, and in that capacity he abolished all toll roads, which was a great benefit to local residents.

Winslow built a two-story home with a stone cellar and then cleared his land. He was doing well and purchased a naphtha gasoline-powered launch, which he pulled home from San Pedro with a team of six horses and a large wagon. The round trip took him nearly three weeks. He was very proud of his boat, boasting that it was unsinkable.

In the spring of 1899, the Nays took some of Cordelia's lady friends boating on Mono Lake. Because several of the ladies developed a severe case of sunburn, Cordelia suggested that Winslow add a canopy to shield them from the sun during future excursions. This he did.

One Sunday morning, a gentle Sierra breeze erupted into a violent windstorm. Now Sierra squalls come up suddenly, first as a gentle breeze, then intensifying within a few hours to a raging wind. When this happens Mono becomes a raging inferno of blowing sand. High, fierce waves, ridged with salt foam, crash around. It's comparable to a small ocean, and Winslow was unaware of this. He'd been waiting for an opportunity to show his friends just how seaworthy the boat was by taking it over to Paoha or Negit, the islands on Mono Lake.[2]

He persuaded five friends to accompany him. One of them, a young fellow in his teens named Johnnie O'Malley, hesitated; but Winslow quieted his fears by convincing him there was no danger. Cordelia walked down to the shore and watched their progress with a spyglass.

The "sailors" started out in high spirits. They'd scarcely started when the boat began to toss violently in the wind. About a mile and half from shore it reached a spot just opposite Hammond's. A horrified Cordelia watched as a mighty gust of wind caught the recently added canopy and capsized the boat.

All on board were lost: Winslow Nay, Frank Schalten, John Mathew, Frank Montrose, J.E. Bean and young Johnnie O'Malley. Only Mr. Bean's body was found.

Mr. Bean was an excellent swimmer, in spite of the fact that he had only one leg. A search team found his body on the edge of Paoha Island. His hands were torn and scratched, as though he had tried to pull himself onto the rugged tufa rocks that line the shore. He is buried at the Lundy cemetery.

---

[2] There are two islands in Mono Lake: *Paoha* ("spirits of the mist"), so-called because of hot water springs which create steam, and *Negit* ("black-winged goose"). (Mono Lake is a haven for Canadian honkers.) These are ancient Paiute names.

The boat was eventually found, in good shape, drifting far along the east side of the Lake. It was even used by others later, and proved to be serviceable.

In the 1950s, Wallis McPherson ran an excursion boat to the Island — the "Venita." Moonlight cruises were a regular feature on balmy summer evenings. One winter, during an intense windstorm, the "Venita" was demolished while beached on the shore, and it was never rebuilt.

The "Venita" nearing Negit Island.

A more recent catastrophe occurred in 1978, when four of Mono's young couples left for an outing to Paoha Island in the late afternoon of Saturday, September 17. They journeyed to the island in two motor boats. After a barbeque, one of the couples returned to shore.

Before dawn on Sunday the wind started to blow, gently at first, then becoming intense during the day, with gusts up to 60 miles an hour.

Friends on shore became uneasy when the remaining couples did not return, and a search was started Sunday evening with no results. It was resumed Monday morning with two deputies and a Sheriff's Patrol boat, along with two helicopters. Five bodies and the overturned fiberglass boat were found at about 9:30 that morning.[3] The sixth victim, John

---

[3] They were identified as Bill Sabo and Elsie Mae Anderson of Yosemite, Philip Defour of Lee Vining, Karen Dudas Butler and her young sister, Cindy Dudas, of Mono City.

Gobel, was recovered on Tuesday morning at the north end of Paoha Island. It was surmised that they attempted to return to the mainland some time on Sunday.

A simple ceremony was held by friends at Mono Lake Park, in sight of Paoha Island where all had perished.

Incidents like these tend to point out how unwise it is to venture out upon Mono Lake, except in the most favorable conditions. On Mono, the slightest error in judgment can prove fatal.

The Gamblers

We anted into the pot of life
as we settled at Mono Lake,
not knowing if Lady Luck would frown
or smile upon us.

We gambled on our crops,
uninsured against the weather
and lucky to break even.

Wagering on the mines,
some held aces and eights.

The joker ran wild in the game of love.

In the end, there were no winners.
Yet, who can say that we are losers?
We persist.

Lily Mathieu La Braque

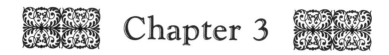

Chapter 3

How Lee Vining Became a Town

When J.B. went down to check on his new "spread," he saw that there was not enough pasture available to nourish his 100 or more cattle and sheep. He would have to grub out large sections of sagebrush to make more pasture, an arduous process. Meanwhile, he knew just the place to graze them. About a mile and a half south, on a high hill overlooking Mono Lake, was a place the farmers called, "Poverty Flat." It had been named that because the dirt was hard-pan,[1] and because the wind blew so fiercely at times. Later, it was renamed "Lakeview."

It was covered with wild pasture and dotted with huge clumps of willows. It was quite suitable for livestock.

In 1900, when I was only a year old, J.B., along with J.S. Cain and Mrs. Condron (the former widow Nay) got land grants from the Federal Government for the Flat. According to the Mono County Courthouse record, it was divided into three parcels.

J.B. got the largest portion — the lower half of the Flat, to the north (just west of the present Lee Vining High School).

Two years later on July 8, 1902, Pete Celini, an Italian farmer, bought the entire property for $800.

Mrs. Condron was paid $200 legal money. J.B. got $500, and J.S. Cain got $100 in gold coins.

Celini retained the land for four years, and in 1906, tempted with the prospect of making a considerable profit, sold it to J.B. and Orilla Anderson for the sum of $2500.

This is when Christian Mattly (Chris) entered the picture. Chris was 12 years old when he arrived here from Switzerland with his bothers, Peter and Hill. The boys went to live with their Uncles Lou and Paul Mattly at Lee Vining Creek. There, they made "Mono Lake Salts," no easy task.

---

[1] *Hard-pan:* Hard packed clay and dirt.

Lee Vining townsite, 1928.

The vats used for boiling the lake water down, were powered by piñon wood, which was cut on the hill to the west of Lee Vining grade. The wood had to be hand sawed, then chopped and loaded on mule-driven wagons.

The Mattlys packaged the salts in half-pint and pint packages, then shipped to it Los Angeles to be sold, where there was a ready market for "Mono Salts."

Years later, Lou and George Williams manufactured the salts, as well as a popular formulated cream which they marketed and sold under the trade name of "Sal-Mono." Mono salts were used for arthritis and athletes' foot, and had numerous other uses. Bathing in the lake water is said to have many beneficial effects.

Chris was an avid believer in the "Salts." As an adult, he drank either a glass of the lake water or dissolved salts every day. Some think he may have drunk too much, because chemicals and salt can settle in the circulatory system, blocking it.

Chris was often seen in the company of his faithful dog "Fritz," an unusual animal, half coyote and half shepherd. Fritz was an excellent hunter, but his career was cut short when his fondness for a farmer's ducks caused him to be shot.

Chris married Anna Keller of Benton in 1922. Anna was a widow, with many children. For several years before Fred Keller died, the Keller family had lived at Benton, where Fred worked as a ranch hand for August Mathieu,[2] on the Mathieu ranch.

The story goes that one day Anna gave a gypsy fortune teller a half dollar to have her hand read. The gypsy solemnly told Anna that her husband would die in a farming accident and that she would lose her eldest son within a year.

Anna scoffed at the dire prediction and ran the woman off the property with her broom.

The gloomy forecast became a reality within the year. The eldest son was killed in a shooting incident and Fred lost his life as he worked, when a wagon he was driving overturned and he was trampled by the panic-stricken horses. The fatherless children were placed in a convent.

When Chris and Anna married, Chris had already bought the Flat from the Andersons for a reported sum of $4000. The children were taken out of the convent and brought to the Basin to live. They were Clare, Vier, Jay, Jim, Anne, Fred, and Verne.

Chris had a weatherbeaten face, a handlebar mustache, and wore glasses. He was short, just 5'5", and his temper was even shorter.

To accommodate his large, new family, Chris had his cousin Hill build him a two-story house at the west end of what is now Third Street. This house is much the same as when it was first built.

Chris and Anna worked hard, with the children helping them. Chris had a large garden (vegetables grew well there). He had ten milk cows, and raised a few sheep and pigs. He sold milk in three- and five-gallon cans. The neighbors dropped by twice a week to pick it up. There were about 50 or 60 chickens. Anna sold eggs and made 25 pounds of butter twice a week, which she sold. Jim Keller vividly recalls churning the butter in a 50-lb. barrel in a creek, by the present Cal-Trans building. It was a big job for a little boy.

As he sat by the fire on cold winter evenings, Chris mulled over the fact that since the Tioga road was built in 1909 to connect with the "Great Sierra Wagon Road," travel over the rough and winding road had been increasing by leaps and bounds. There was a practical side to his otherwise dreamy nature; and now one of his dreams began to take shape.

You might say that he had a "vision."

He invited his relatives and neighbors to one of his famous Canasta parties, hinting that he would be discussing an issue of great importance.

---

[2] Father of Pete, John, Frank and August.

Chris Mattly, founder of Lee Vining.

Anna Mattly and baby.

The Keller family in 1916, at hog-killing time.

They pestered him for details; but he gave nary a clue, saying it was a secret.

Toward the end of the evening, as Anna fortified the curious guests with refreshments, Chris revealed his "great" plan.

He began by saying that before long he expected there would be a great increase in travel through Yosemite. (The road, in fact, had only recently been improved to accommodate touring cars.) He explained that with this in mind, he planned to sell the lower portion of his ranch to Bob Currie, a butcher who owned a slaughterhouse up Lee Vining Creek.

Basinites in attendance were Pearl and Jake Mattly, the Hess brothers (also from Switzerland), the Donellys, Montroses, and I, George La Braque.

They listened, dubiously, as he went on to say that he intended to subdivide the upper portion of his property, and that he was giving them the first chance to buy lots. He told them to go home and talk it over and to let him know what they decided. One man timidly asked, "What will you call it?"

Leroy Vining
of Vining's Rancho

Chris tugged thoughtfully at his mustache, then replied, "I will call it Lee Vining."

The others had heard the story of Leroy Vining, who had come into the Basin with his brother Dick, on a quest for gold in 1856, and who had died around 1870.

The brothers were from La Porte, Indiana, originally. They traveled from Mariposa into Coarse Gold at Yosemite to mine and trap.

They worked first as hardrock miners for the "Sheepherder Mine" at the top of Tioga Pass.[3] The mine failed, but reports of gold at Monoville by a Lieutenant Moore encouraged them to stick around. They hired an

---

[3] *Tioga:* An Iroquois name meaning "where it forks." The road over the Tioga Pass was originally an ancient Indian footpath. The Great Sierra Wagon Road was the first finished portion. Today, the road is a sleek, two-lane highway, bordered by Alpine meadows, granite peaks, timber stands, and glistening snowcaps.

Indian guide to take them down through Bloody Canyon,[4] by way of Mono Pass, panning for gold as they followed Walker Creek. Dick Vining parted with Leroy and drifted north. Leroy built a large sluice box at Rescue Creek (directly opposite the present town). He was recovering a sizeable amount of gold dust, when he learned of the rich placers being discovered at Mono Diggings, a few miles to the north. He established a claim, which is said to have been one of the richest there.

Leroy was well acquainted with the fact that mining made a man mighty thirsty. He opened a makeshift "saloon" in the foothills, at the mining camp named "Monoville." The settlement included several hotels, a Chinese laundry, grocery store, barber shop, and livery stable.

Because of his colorful speech and important "airs," he was called "Captain Vining." He did well, until a heavy snow caved in the roof of his establishment. As the miners were vacating the premises for a new bonanza in Aurora, Leroy took the little stake he had saved and bought property at the base of Tioga Pass (in the vicinity of the present Senior Citizen camp). He built a small cabin near the creek for his Paiute wife and himself, and then started a sawmill. His spread, which included a small meadow, became known as "Vining's Rancho."

"Vining's Rancho" is identified on Clayton's map of Esmeralda and Mono Counties. Clayton refers to Lee Vining River, although the name Rescue Creek was given this stream by Von Schmidt, who did the official survey in 1856.

Leroy was a rugged outdoorsman, and handy with a gun. A gun, however, proved to be his undoing. One day, around 1870, as he was hauling lumber on the rough road from Bodie to Aurora, the buckboard jolted suddenly, throwing his gun out of the holster on his hip, and causing it to discharge accidently. In a few minutes, Leroy Vining was dead.

His wife went back to her people, and later, Albert Silvester picked up "Vining's Rancho" for back taxes.

Chris Mattly's guests all knew this story. They left with their heads swimming at the unexpected proposition; and in the days that followed, others, especially Chris's Uncle Jake, pleaded with Chris to forget his brainstorm. But Chris had made up his mind.

---

[4] *Bloody Canyon:* The canyon might have been named because of the bloody battles between the Kuzedika Paiute and the Yosemite (Yokut) Indians over control of the brine shrimp "lots" at Mono Lake. (The Yokuts considered the brine shrimp to be a delicacy.) However, in John Muir's essay on "Peaks and Glaciers of the High Sierras," he claims it may have been derived from the red color of the sides, or from the bloody stains left by mules and horses whose hooves were cut by the sharp rocks on the path.

Chris Mattly, Founder of Lee Vining

A public meeting was held to discuss the idea. Some Basinites were not sure they wanted a town. Most thought it was a huge joke; but soon the idea caught on and was accepted.

Chris's first move was to hire Charlie Fulton, the stage and mail driver, who was also the Mono County Surveyor, to survey the townsite.

The upper half of the property was solidly overgrown with high, tough willows that had to be chopped and hacked out of the way before surveying could proceed.

Chris hired some local lads to help Charlie: August Hess, Don Mattly, the Carrington brothers, and Jim Keller, his own stepson. Jim pulled the chain, packed a hatchet, and hauled the stakes.

Anna and Chris saw a chance to establish a school for the children. There were two schools in the Basin at this time. Mono Lake School, to the north, across from Mono Inn, and the Crater School, to the south, at Farrington Meadow.

Early one morning Anna marched to the little rise at the southwest part of the townsite. There, with her children trailing behind her, she "walked off" the portion she wanted set aside for the school. It was not an accurately measured piece of property; indeed, the finished division of the town into lots had a patch-work effect. The lots which Anna walked off, and which she and Chris deeded to Mono County for a school, were numbers 7, 8, 9, 10, and 11. The Mattlys added the stipulation that if the school were to be discontinued or moved, the property would revert to their heirs.

The Lee Vining Grammar School — much expanded and improved — occupies this land today.

The townsite caught on. The Courthouse records show that the first lots were sold in 1926, for $50 per lot.

The buyers were: Guy Carrington (2 lots),[5] Glenn Mattly (2 lots),[6] Bill Hess (3 lots),[7] Gus Hess (3 lots),[8] Margaret Calhoun (1 lot).[9]

---

[5] Grocery store.

[7] First garage.

[8] Gas station-bar-restaurant.

[9] First post office, barber shop, and bakery.

In 1927, lots were bought by Bill Donelly (1 lot), Anna Currie (1 lot),[10] Peter Gilli (2 lots),[11] Bill Parmalee (1 lot),[12] Albert Silvester (1 lot), Lawrence L. Bodle (1 lot), Margaret Calhoun (1 lot), Henry Heavrin (1 lot), James Green (1 lot), and F.A. Mansfield (1 lot).

In 1930, lots were purchased by George Mitchell, Gus Hess, Frank Donelly,[13] William Currie, and me, George La Braque.[14]

As usual, "inflation" arrived, and the next lots sold for $150-$200. Amazingly enough, the going price for a lot in the townsite today ranges from a low of $18,000 to a high of $25,000 — provided any can be found, that is.

Chris, having a large stake in the school, served for many years as a board member, custodian, and jack-of-all-trades, which helped keep the school running smoothly.

Nora A. Archer, first Superintendent of Schools.

Mechanics Bill and Gus Hess drove schoolbus. Note Dodge truck in background.

Other board members were Bill Banta,[15] Gus Hess, and Jim Stewart, who was President of the board for many years.

Mrs. Nora Archer, a widow with several children, was the first superintendent of schools. She attended nearly every board meeting, and had very precise standards and high ideals.

The first teacher was Miss Young. She lived on the second floor of the Mattly house, and later moved to lower Lee Vining Creek, where she

[10] Currie's Meat Market.

[11] El Mono Hotel.

[12] Restaurant.

[13] Restaurant, the O.K. Cafe.

[14] Shell Station, La Braque Motel.

[15] Bill's youngest son, Don, is—and has been for many years—chairman of the Lee Vining Utility District.

could house all her felines in a very large house. These were strays that she simply could not resist — and there were *dozens* of them. She lived there until her death.

The second teacher was Mrs. Lottie Van Allstyn. Oh, Yes!! I remember her well. My daughter Lily was in the first grade (1929), and quite a mischief. I vividly recall the welts raised on her bare legs, put there by Lottie's willow switches.

It was a very sad thing for Chris and the children when Anna died in 1925, giving birth to their son Leo. Leo was sent to relatives in Bakersfield. Chris kept the others at home with him.

At this time there was no road through the townsite. From the south, the highway took off in the vicinity of the present Lee Vining airport, down over the hill north of Cramasco's truck garden (now Dondero's), along Mono Lake. When you reached the bridge over Lee Vining Creek, *on this side*, you made a sharp left following the creek upward, across a bridge, and stopping at Anderson's (later Curry's). Then you entered town by foot. If you wanted to go on to Tioga Lodge, you'd continue *northward* (instead of turning left up the canyon). Later, a Forest Service road was built above town. It originated at the Lee Vining Dam and continued high on the hill beyond town, coming out at Tioga Lodge. You had to double back, so to speak, to get into Lee Vining proper.

As mentioned earlier, Bob Currie operated the slaughterhouse. He had a hardworking, well-liked Paiute named Jaspar Jack working for him as slaughterer. Bob sold his meat at the small meat market he'd built next to Glen Mattly's store (Lee Vining Market today).

Bob had the first electricity in Lee Vining. He paid $40 for the first pole, to bring electricity to his business. The sewer system went in many years later, and is one of the oldest sewer systems in existence.

Because Bob needed water in the worst way, his friend Bill Banta helped him shovel a ditch of some 50 yards to bring water down from an open ditch that took the water to the school.

Bill Banta was no stranger to the Basin. He had come into Mono Basin from Owens Valley in 1918, to peddle vegetables. The demand was so great that he soon had five trucks operating. The vegetables were grown and trucked in from the rich farming community of Bishop. Bill would often find his payment in chickens, eggs, and so forth; and a few times Paiutes paid him in gold coins.

Around 1930, the first water line was brought in at a point where the Blaver residence now stands. Fred Silva was the foreman. Paiute lads who worked on the line were Harry Tom, Frank Sam, Billy Williams,

Lee Vining Barbeque — 1930. (L. to r.: Caroline Curry, Gus and Lula Hess, Mary Donnelly, Keller boys, John Dondero, Bill Hess, Jim Duffy, Bob Currie and sons.)

Billy Abe, and Dick Charlie. It was put in with a plow, a team of horses, and, mostly, a lot of shoveling.

Bill and Gus Hess, together with Guy Carrington, put in the pipes and copper fittings. These were hooked up to all businesses and homes.

The new waterline didn't work at all well, and that's an understatement. The reason is that at the south end of town, on the hill, a 4-inch line was installed. This narrowed to a 2-inch line in the middle of town, and to a 1½-inch line at the lower half. The lower half of town was often without a drop of water. A very frustrating problem..

The town made do with this for many years until the school board and townspeople agreed that this water system was obsolete. A real water system, with uniform pressure, was needed. In emergencies the original system was not dependable.

Plans were drawn up for a new waterline; and the townspeople called on the County of Mono for financial aid. The next step was to circulate a petition. The signers agreed to pay a 6% school tax. The amount of money needed to be raised for the project was $3500.

Bill Banta bought the water pipe from the City of Los Angeles for 25¢

per foot. The County money was given as a loan, and there was some free help from the Federal government as well.

The townspeople borrowed one tractor, and the City of Los Angeles loaned them another. The line was completed in 1940, and everyone paid $40 for each hook-up.

Bill Banta had two lots, as well as the grocery store he had bought from Glen Mattly.[16] He gave the Edison Company an easement for the electricity to come into the town through his property. This line is still called the "Banta" line by the company.

Around 1927, the persuasive Chris had convinced Gus and Bill Hess to move their garage into town from the Tioga Lodge location. They did so, taking in Guy Carrington as a partner. There was a method in his madness, so to speak, as Chris usually had several broken down trucks in need of repair; and the brothers were excellent mechanics.

Their first garage was at the north end of town. Later they established a permanent garage and gas station at the south end of town. Gus' oldest son, August, is still in business there.

Gus and Bill married two Paiute sisters, Lula and Mildred Charlie from Owens Valley; and both had large families.

With their large Dodge trucks, Bill and Gus moved the building for the school in from Mono Mills. We Basinites would have occasion to call upon these trucks for much of the heavy work done in the Basin. For many years, Gus and Bill hauled the heavy mining timbers up to the Log Cabin Mine, an extremely difficult task because of a steep, rough grade that had several hairpin turns. Even though they had to proceed at a snail's pace, they always made it.

Chris and young Gus had been good friends. Gus was kind of his "protégé." They worked together for the good of the town for many years. At Chris's death, Gus took over many town matters, becoming town "Constable." Gus has sometimes been called the "Father of Lee Vining."

Up to the 1930s, there had been little "law and order" in the townsite. Mike Lazovitch of Bodie built and ran the "hot spot of relaxation and bamboozlery, Bodie Mike's Bar and Restaurant.[17]

An Italian, Julio Zuninio, owned Julio's Saloon, next door; and Bill Fuller ran the adjoining Sez Bill Cafe. Their patrons enjoyed "wild and woolly" times, with an occasional murder or shooting scrape to liven things up.

---

[16] Lee Vining Market (Barsi).

[17] Bodie Mike's Bar & Restaurant is now owned and operated by Jim and Edna Nicely.

Chef Bill Fuller of "Sez Bill's Cafe."

One cold, blistery day in 1934, Chris went out woodcutting to Deadman with a four-horse team. As he started home, the horses started running wildly, for some reason. The wagonload of wood overturned, with all the wood falling on top of Chris. When he did not return all night, Pearl and Glen Mattly went looking for him.

They found Chris very cold, dazed and smashed up, with broken ribs and other injuries. He had also suffered a slight stroke. He lived until 1937, but he never completely recovered from the accident.

Many of these old friends of mine played leading roles in the formation of Lee Vining.

 # Chapter 4

The Sandpiper

After my mother had recovered from the shock that J.B. had actually won the Nay ranch in the poker game, she excitedly began making preparations for the move to our new "spread." We sold our old place to William Dickerson, and soon we were off to the "Nay" ranch at the foot of Lee Vining grade, close to the lake shore.

The once cultivated meadows are, in fact, still visible, as are the remains of our home and its stone cellar.

If you look several hundred yards to the left of the homesite, you'll

Remains of our home, former Nay ranch.

Jerome's "tufa rock cooler," on the Nay ranch.

see a large tufa[1] rock about 15 feet high, with a natural hollow. When we lived there, this rock had an ice cold spring gurgling up from the ground under it. It became our refrigerator. There was a hole in the top of the rock for ventilation, and a natural shelf where eggs, butter, and milk could be kept cool. We hung mutton and beef there, and made a makeshift door to keep everything safe from marauders.

The rock is unchanged today, though the spring has vanished. At times it shelters unexpected overnight guests; and in the spring, wild roses bloom beside the door.

My parents had sheep and cattle. Mother, barefoot, tended the sheep. J.B. raised alfalfa, hay, and vegetables. As they were both busy, they

---

[1] *Tufa:* a white, calcified rock-like formation formed by precipitation of limestone from incoming fresh-water springs under what, ages ago, was the vast surface of Mono Lake. As the incoming fresh water blended with the highly mineralized lake water, the lime was deposited through a chemical action, forming tubular towers around the incoming fresh water stream. These deposits, built up over many years, form Mono Lake's famous tufa "towers." Many of the towers now above the water's edge have fresh water springs flowing out of their sides or basis. Others, whose tops are barely visible, have fresh water flowing up through the original central tube and rising up above the lake surface.

hired a *mahalia* (a Paiute word for "servant" pronounced "may-hay-lee") to take care of the house and be a nursemaid for me, "little Georgie." I was about four years old then, and really a handful.

The *mahalia* never banished me unless I was extra ornery, but one day I threw a tantrum and upstairs I went. After a while she noticed that it was much too quiet. She came upstairs to see what I was doing. Well, I wasn't there.

At first she thought I was hiding, but when she saw the open window, she knew I had jumped to the ground and run away. She ran to the fields where my folks were working, hoping I was there. Then, the three of them began to search for the "little mischief."

Mother knew I liked to play down by the shore, so they started out in that direction. The *mahalia* found my trail and saw me lying, motionless and half drowned. Fearing the worst, she shook me hard, but I couldn't respond.

What had happened after I'd escaped from my room was this: I had found and chased a crippled sandpiper along the beach. But each time I got close, the bird swam farther out onto the lake. I followed it into the deep water, but I could never get my hands on it. I fell into a hole and water rushed over my head.

Everything went black. I thought I was going to die because the lake water stung my eyes and I had to keep them shut. I couldn't breathe. Somehow, I bobbed to the surface and, opening my eyes, glimpsed the shoreline. With much effort I reached the beach, where I collapsed.

J.B. worked desperately to revive me, and in the process I upchucked must of the briny, mineralized water. (Mono Lake water is not known to aid the digestion.)

This narrow escape did little to dampen my spirits, and in a couple of hours I was running around just as feisty as ever. My folks were shaken up and determined to keep a closer watch on me.

Our ranch might have continued to prosper, but the San Francisco earthquake in 1906 had a disastrous effect on those of us with property close to the shore. For several weeks after the quake, Mono Lake rose 30 feet or more, covering fences, pastures, and finally, the ground floor of our house.

A large spring or source of water had evidently opened in the lake's bottom. J.B. was so disgusted to see his hard work go for naught that he sold the ranch back to Jack Hammond for $4000.

We left by way of the Bodie road, by horse and wagon, with my Aunt Mary accompanying us on horseback for several miles. She had been

The Hayworths with one of their children, my mother, Agnes, and me (at the wheel), El Reno, Oklahoma.

very good to me, and I shed bitter tears as she left us to return to the ranch.

Hello, Oklahoma

J.B. bought a strawberry farm in Garden Grove; but other Lake settlers, like our good friends the Hayworths, joined a wagon train headed for Oklahoma.

Our strawberry crop was badly destroyed by the abundant sand fleas, however, and so J.B. sold the place. Once again we picked up our belongings and we took a train to join the Hayworths, who were now living in El Reno, Oklahoma.

The trip was not without its humor, I recall. As was customary, when we boarded the train we carried a large picnic basket to tide us over to our destination. Our fellow passengers had already begun eating their lunches when we commenced eating ours. The next minute, all seats close were vacant. You see, J.B. was especially fond of limburger cheese, and Agnes had brought along a huge slab.

As my mother saw the sudden exodus of passengers, she was terribly embarrassed. "This is the worst mistake we ever made, bringing that cheese along!" she berated my father, who blissfully ignored the tongue-lashing as he ate with gusto, lit up his pipe, and declared it *très bon* ("very good"). Mother, he said, was a fine cook.

The year was about 1906. We lived with the Hayworths and their five children for some time. Avis and Luva Hayworth, who were about my age, were my favorite playmates. Mr. Hayworth, a Methodist minister and an excellent carpenter, helped my father build three houses. One to live in, and two to rent as an investment. We were happy to move into our own house. Things began returning to normal.

J.B. went to work on the railroad and resumed his cardplaying. I was about eight years old, and left on my own a good deal of the time. I was mischievous, strong-willed, and on my way to becoming a problem.

Chapter 5

My Life with the Fathers

(I was cautioned before writing this book not to tell everything I know and saw, as it could hurt somebody or myself. However, like other things in my life, I am going to write it as I felt and saw it, only changing some names to protect living persons.)
George La Braque, Sr.

In El Reno, at the age of nine, I put in my time selling newspapers and fighting. Most of my fights were with Negro children. One of them, Fanny, used to chase me all the time. She was a lot bigger than I, and one day when she chased me home, I took my air gun and shot her in the leg. Believe me, all hell broke loose. Her family sent the police to our house. My folks had to do *something* with me, so they sent me off, some miles away, to a boy's school run by Catholic priests. My experiences there will follow me to my grave. The head Father was a very mean man.

Every day we had little white navy beans to eat, not without flies. Every morning at daybreak we got up and went to Mass. Every day some of us were savagely disciplined with rubber hoses by the Fathers. Too many times I was one of the unlucky ones.

We children ranged in age from about eight to eighteen. We were beaten for smoking, fighting, and running away — mong other things. We spent a lot of time figuring out ways to escape.

One day during a picnic in the woods, three of us ran off. We were caught, and once again took an awful beating from the Fathers.

Most of the boys had been sent there because we'd had some trouble at home, or because our folks were too poor to take care of us. Many of the boys had been beaten at home. I had not. It was the *way* in which the Fathers beat us which was so bad . . .

One day, I got into a fight with a Jewish boy whom we all picked on. But that day, to my surprise, he turned on me and beat me up. Of course,

The three of us in El Reno, 1908.

we were taken before the Fathers who gave us a terrific beating with rubber hoses. Another day, I fought with an Indian boy who used to hit and kick me all the time. He was bigger than I, and I was afraid of him. This time I turned on him and threw him to the ground. He pulled a big nail out of his pocket and tried to get at my face. I put my hands on his throat and squeezed until he quit moving. Other boys pulled me off, and someone brought him to by throwing buckets of water on him.

Now, there was hell going on, and the Fathers really gave me a terrible beating, in their usual way.

For a while I got into no further trouble, but one day the Fathers caught me smoking again. (We got our tobacco from the big boys, one way or another.) This time I was really angry and started to plan a runaway by myself, figuring I'd have a better chance alone. I was right.

On my way to Mass one morning, I noticed a break in the lattice work under the porch of a building that we passed each day. I figured I could make this my escape hole. Some time later, as we all lined up for Mass, I managed to be last in line; and as we marched ahead I ducked in the hole and stayed there until everybody else was at prayers. Then I ran off across the field as fast as I could, saying my own kind of prayer as I ran. About the time I reached the school fence, I heard bloodhounds barking.

Three dogs, kept there to track runaways, were trailing me. Knowing I didn't stand a chance trying to run, I started running *toward* them. That surprised the dogs so much they didn't know what to do. I wasn't a stranger to them. Prior to this I had fed them bread crusts; and as they milled curiously round me I petted them. I threw sticks for them. One dog especially thought it great fun to fetch and bring the stick back to me. They followed me for a while, chasing squirrels. Scattering out, they finally left me.

Soon I spotted two Brothers coming my way. They were young, active men and I didn't think I could outrun them. Brothers and Fathers had a habit of walking with their head down; and on this day that habit was just right for me. I jumped behind a big old stump and they passed by without ever raising their heads.

I had no idea of where to go; my only thought was to get away.

Watching some squirrels carrying nuts from the trees on that warm fall day, I became very thirsty. I noticed a telephone line, and I was old enough to know that it went somewhere. I followed it and soon came upon an old shack. Hearing a noise, I went to the back, where a very tall and thin lady was pulling up a bucket out of a well. She worked a windlass, but it was too heavy for her and so I offered to help. We got the bucket up and she gave me a drink of water. I drank so fast that she told me to be careful, to drink slowly, as she could see I was thirsty.

Now something strange happened to me then which also happened years later: the woman asked if I was hungry and I said, "No." (I was starving!!) I had always been shy, and I told her I had already eaten at the wagon I had left a little while ago. She asked me what I meant. I told her I had got out of my folks' wagon to go and look for nuts, and now I couldn't find my way back. She thought that was terrible and asked a lot of questions, but I could see she believed my story.

The woman told me to go back to town, as my folks were probably there, looking for me. I should follow the old road back of her home until I got there. I did, thinking what a fool I'd been not to take her up on her offer of food.

Some people passed by in wagons and on horseback. They gave me strange looks, but none spoke to me nor I to them. Finally, I saw some buildings ahead and kids playing in the streets. It was late as I entered the town, scared to death and not knowing what to do next. A kid threw a half-eaten piece of banana candy on the ground and when no one was looking I picked it up and ate it. It sure tasted good.

I walked and walked, and came to a blacksmith shop. The man there had on a black cap. He was very tall, with a pleasant face and good features. I sat on a box by the door, watching him work on red-hot iron. For a long time neither of us spoke. By this time it was nearly dark, and he took off his apron and began putting away his tools.

"Kid," he said, "What are you doing here? Why aren't you going home?"

I told him I had no home here. He asked, "Why not?" I told him the following story. I will never forget it! I told him that my parents, brothers, sisters, and I were traveling together from Oklahoma City with another wagon, and that somehow my folks must have thought that when they left this town I was on the *other* wagon. The blacksmith told me not to worry. He saw how scared I was and told me to take the box outside and wait for my folks. They'd be back for me any minute. I was about ready to leave when he came to see if I was still there. He thought it was strange that my folks hadn't shown up, as it was now completely dark.

He said for me to come with him, and as we walked, he questioned me. I answered carefully. We arrived at a hotel, where the blacksmith talked to the lady in charge. A little girl my age was there. She and I talked together, and I remembered her name for years. The lady took me upstairs to a little room and a bed, telling me I could sleep there for the night. Soon there was a hot supper ready. It tasted so good after the Fathers' meals. I was too bashful to eat as much as I wanted, and I left the table still hungry.

The next two days I spent playing with the little girl. She let me use her skates. We became good friends. I was having a good time, but I knew I ought to get away from there. Thing was, *I didn't know where to go.* I didn't know in what direction El Reno was, and as far as I knew, it might be 200 miles away. The couple who ran the hotel were puzzled that my folks still hadn't turned up. On the third day I told the little girl that if she would not tell on me, I'd tell her why I was there. She promised, and I told her about my escape. Very late that afternoon, a buckboard with two Fathers in it stopped at the hotel, perhaps a block away from where we were playing. Quickly taking off and returning her skates, I pointed to the Fathers and said goodbye. I started to run, but the girl ran after me and grabbed my arm, crying and pleading with me not to run away again: "You'll starve to death! You'll get lost and die!" I was crying too, not from fear, but because I hated to leave her.

The Fathers had seen us. They grabbed me by the arm, and led me away. The girl's mother talked to me very kindly and told me not to be scared. She didn't understand that I was crying because the two days there had been a kind of heaven, and I was going back into a kind of hell.

So once again I was headed for the Fathers. The two who had come for me sat me between them. As soon as the people were out of sight, they stopped and one of them took out a rope hidden under his robe. They put me in the back of the buckboard, tying my hands and feet, and left me lying there. They gave the whip to the team and then we were *really* off at a run. I was bouncing up and down, and whenever we'd hit holes in the road, there was no way I could break my fall. It took more than an hour to get back to the Fathers. I wasn't told what lay ahead for me. Although I was prepared for another beating, in spite of all my previous experience with the Fathers' rubber hose, the beating I now took from them truly shocked me. The method was the usual, but this time it lasted much longer because I refused to say, "No" when asked if I would try to run away again.

Listen to how they beat me in those days: I had to lie over a Father's left leg while he sat on a chair. With his left hand he grabbed my privates, while with the other he beat my back and legs with a double hose. Two Fathers took turns beating me, and my privates were squeezed so hard that my testicles hurt for days afterward. They finally saw that I wouldn't say "No," and when they released me, I fell. I couldn't stand or walk. The Fathers carried me to my room and left me.

Later that night a strange thing happened. One of the Fathers who had beaten me came for me and led me into the dining room. I was the only kid at the table, as it was very late at night. He served me eggs and meat, things I had never eaten there before. Afterward, I was taken back to my room. Not a word was spoken between us.

I was so sore that I couldn't sleep all night, and I kept telling myself that I would make a better escape next time. All the while, I had it in my mind to let my mother and father know what I was suffering; but I had no way to contact them. I was so young, I couldn't figure out a way. The next morning another surprise was waiting for me.

A Brother came to my room, saying I would not have to go to Mass or school anymore. There was no explanation. For several days I played a little, but very little because of the welts on my back and legs. Kids would ask me why I hadn't been to Mass or school, but I didn't know either.

One day, a Brother came to my room, picked up my belongings, and led me to the reception room. My mother was there, waiting to take me home. The Fathers hauled us to the train in the buckboard. It wasn't until we were safely away from the place, that I answered the question my mother had been asking over and over: "Why can you hardly walk?" She was very angry.

The train ride to El Reno took several hours, and I was glad to be home again. J.B. came home from his day's work on the railroad just as my mother got all my clothes off and was spreading ointment on my welts. When she told him what had happened to me, my father wanted to go out to the Fathers' school then and there, for a confrontation; but my mother talked him out of it.

I was sick and sore for many days, and never in my life have I forgotten those beatings the Fathers gave me. For years I hated the sight of a Father or a priest.

One day, a Sister came to our house to see my mother. I ran from the house. That night, my mother told me I would be going to the Sisters' school in town. I stormed about this until my father quieted me down, telling me that it would be completely different from the Fathers' school. My mother took me there next morning.

At first, I was mad and as ornery as any kid could be. I wouldn't talk to any of the Sisters, nor would I do anything they asked me to do. It seemed strange to me how the other kids would swarm happily around them. Sister Marie taught my class. She never raised her voice. I would do things on purpose to see if I could get her to yell at me, but she never scolded me for anything. Little by little, I began to talk to her. She always had a smile and a kind word for me. I began to study and take my books home. At the end, I couldn't do enough for her. I grew to love her very much, and to this day, I believe that I learned more there than I ever had before. I still have the little catechism book Sister Marie gave me.

It was 1910, and I was now 11 years old. Agnes and J.B. were not getting along well; and besides, Agnes was homesick. J.B. decided it would be a good idea if she would take me home to the ranch in Mono Basin. It would be a much better environment for a young boy, they decided, especially compared to the back streets of El Reno.

I hated to leave Sister Marie, my friends, and especially my father. I did not know it then, but it would be years before I set eyes on J.B. again.

This time, Mother and I took the train bound for Carson City, Nevada. Agnes mailed a tearful letter to J.B. at Salt Lake City, telling him she was already sorry she had left. But it was too late for regrets.

Chapter 6

Avalanche at Jordan

My mother and I spent the winter months of 1910-11 in Carson City with her father, who had remarried.

One day, grandfather Charlie rushed home from town with some exciting news that was also very frightening. "All hell broke loose at Mono Lake yesterday." He went on to say that there had been a tremendous avalanche four miles west of Mono Lake at the Southern Sierra Power Company's plant at Jordan, near the base of Copper Mountain. It was said to be the worst ever experienced in Mono Basin. Rescue operations were underway to locate survivors — if any. The rescue operations were being hampered by blizzard conditions.

A fine powder snow had begun to fall in December, changing to a sleety, wet snow the first part of January, and finally ending on January 16. Residents of Mono Basin were greatly relieved, but not for long. An intense cold spell followed the storm, accompanied by a dense "Mono fog." Mono Basin was transformed into a solid cake of ice.[1]

On February 22, the snow resumed, continuing for three weeks. It ended on March 10.

When the power went off at midnight, Bodie was the first to take action. (Bodie was the closest town and Southern Sierra's main office was there.)

Two power company employees were sent on skis over to Jordan. They were bucking fifty-mile-an-hour winds, blizzards, and loose-flying snow. As the repairmen reached the top of the ridge they expected to see the power house and nearby cottages; but to their surprise, nothing was visible but a tremendous mountain of snow. The snowslide had wiped out the entire settlement.

Immediately after this news reached the Bodie Power Company, a messenger was rushed out to spread the news to Bodie's many saloons. In

---

[1] Adapted from *Mineral County Independent News,* Hawthorne, Nevada, February 26, 1969. Related by Joe Scanavino.

the dim candlelight he called at the top of his voice: "Attention everyone, I have news from the repair crew." Everything went quiet. "Jordan Power plant was struck by a snowslide. It's completely wiped out. Seven men and one woman are buried under the snow."

These words sent chills through everyone who heard. Even hard, tough miners wilted back into their chairs and dropped their heads with a few words of prayer. They knew from past experience that a snowslide could be deadly.

Nothing was more important than getting to Jordan, and in less than an hour a hundred men were skiing out of Bodie.

The blizzard was raging, and at different points, thirty or so of the men had to turn back, due to exhaustion or sprained muscles. The rest continued, arriving at the Scanavino ranch (a halfway point and stage stop) at 6 a.m. After a big breakfast and four hours' rest, the remaining 70 men continued on, although some had developed colds and frostbite. Twenty-eight feet of snow fell on Bodie, and over 25 feet fell at Jordan. Eight feet of snow covered the sagebrush and fence posts at my grandmother Mary Filosena's ranch.

At midnight, on March 7 — 12:01 to be exact — "all hell broke loose." It was the largest snowslide ever: over a mile long, half a mile wide, and 18 to 22 feet deep. When the entire east side of Copper Mountain finally slid off, an estimated 4000 tons of snow piled down around the base.

The big slide cleaned out everything. The power house, four cottages, and hundred-year-old trees, which were sheared off right at the ground and then carried 500 feet.

The power plant had been put into operation in the fall of 1910. It transmitted power to Bodie and Aurora, ending at the Wonder Mine in Aurora. Prior to the Jordan facility, the Green Creek Power plant had been used to transmit power to Bodie. The Green Creek power line was 13 miles long. It consisted of two wires which led directly to the Standard Mine at Bodie. Its completion in 1893 was a major event. In fact, when Clarence Peck threw the switch that activated the first power to Bodie, the news was flashed around the world.

The force and speed of the Jordan avalanche was tremendous. An electric transformer inside the power house, which stood over 15 feet and weighed over 20 tons, skidded vertically over 300 feet. It was still in a vertical position when it stopped skidding.

Other men from nearby communities arrived to join the Bodie group in digging at the location of the avalanche.

It was −28 °F. during the rescue operations, and wherever they dug, small slides kept coming their way. When that occurred, those shoveling

Green Creek Power House, 1893. Clarence Peck activates switch sending electricity to Bodie for the first time.

ran to safety, returning later to dig out their tools before continuing their grim task.

The six bodies that were found first had all been Power Company employees and were in the power plant at the time of the slide. They skidded the 500 feet along with the power house machinery, and were buried alive.

At 2:23 that afternoon of March 10, the wall of one of the cottages was located. Mrs. and Mrs. Mason (also Power Company employees) were known to have been sleeping there at the time of the slide.

The first indication of life was the faint, whimpering noise of a dog. Shep, the Mason's dog, was pulled out and given first aid. He was terribly cold and shivering.

The digging continued, and suddenly, low and painful groans were heard. The Masons had been found.

Mr. Mason had been killed instantly by a huge concrete slab — part of the power house — that weighed several tons. Because his body was pinned against Mrs. Mason's leg, she could not move. A large trunk on her side of the bed, four inches higher than the bed itself, had saved her from the direct weight of the concrete. She and the dog had just four inches in which to move and breathe.

It had been 62½ hours since the snowslide struck. They gave Mrs. Mason first aid, but her leg was badly infected. Ten men on skis hitched themselves to a toboggan and wasted no time pulling her to the Conway ranch two miles away.

The Fred Mattly ranch at Jordan, as skiers prepare to pull Mrs. Mason to Conway ranch.

The trip was completed in 37 minutes. Mrs. Conway, a trained nurse, realized that Mrs. Mason had gangrene and must be taken to the Bodie Hospital right away. John Conway instructed his blacksmith to fix steel runners to a toboggan and equipped the sled with eight pulling ropes. They knew it might take as long as three days to reach Bodie.

Louis De Chambeau, the ski-maker, brought all his extra skis, and along with many Indian men, volunteered his help on this life-and-death run.

Mrs. Mason left the ranch at 4 a.m. on March 11, pulled by a team of 48 expert skiers. They left early to take advantage of the frozen snow.

Mrs. Agnes Mason, Who Was Snatched From Awful Death

NIGHT OF TERROR
IN SNOW SLIDE

Woman Whose Husband Was Killed Tells of Terrible Experience

OAKLAND, April 1.—Rescued from a grave of snow and the timbers of a demolished cabin, where she lay pinned 60 hours beside the dead body of her husband, with her shepherd dog keeping her awake by licking her face and barking, Mrs. Agnes Mason is at the Fabiola hospital convalescing from the serious illness which followed.

The slide which killed Mason came thundering down from the smooth granite slopes of the Sierra in Mono county, wiped out the new power plant of the Hydro electric company and the cabins surrounding it and killed six men besides Mason.

"I don't know how or when it happened," said Mrs. Mason tonight. "Shep, the dog, awakened me, and I found that I could not move. I called to my husband, but he did not answer. My right arm was pinned across my chest. My right knee and heel were across my husband. I found that I could move my head a little, but when I raised my face an inch and a half I struck the timbers of what had been the roof of our cabin. How I knew that my husband was dead, I can not tell. The snow was everywhere about, but the heat of the dog and my own breathing made it warm and I did not suffer from the cold.

"But when my husband grew cold beside me—then I knew—" and tears came to her eyes.

"I talked to Shep and he tried to talk back. He whined and howled and barked and scratched at the snow and at the timbers.

"I must have been unconscious at times, for it didn't seem long before I heard men walking on the snow overhead. I called as loud as I could and told Shep to bark. You should have heard him. Quickly they dug down where we were. They said the snow was eight feet deep overhead.

"Well, they got us out at last. We had to stay there in the shanty several days while 20 men were breaking a road through the snow to Bodie. They built a sled and carried me to the Conway ranch, where we had a doctor. My grandfather, Henry Thornton, was notified, and he came up from Arizona and arranged for me to come here."

From *San Francisco Call Bulletin*, April 2, 1911

Maude Conway, John's niece, went along with the team to help care for the patient. She too was an expert skier.

Sixteen-year-old Steve Scanavino was sent on ahead to the next spread, the Scanavino ranch, to make sure his folks would be ready to feed 75 people. A steer and two hogs were butchered, and the food was on the table when the caravan arrived at 3:30 p.m. They had been traveling 11 hours.

Just past midnight on March 12, everyone got up to eat a large breakfast. Lunches were packed on a second toboggan, and so were a coffee pot, homemade stove, and a thirty-gallon drum of water. This sled was pulled by a team of six skiers. The caravan pulled out at 1 a.m.

At −16°F., the weather was calm and icy. The Indian men saved several hours' time by taking over the pulling on snowshoes whenever they came to a hill, as the skis would keep sliding backward.

The townspeople of Bodie worked day and night from the other end, with horses and shovels, to open the road at Butcher Flat and Sugar Loaf grade through 20 feet of snow. When the man-powered toboggan met up with them, the patient was transferred to a sleigh, pulled by a snowshoed team of horses.

Mrs. Mason was soon in the Bodie Hospital, but the gangrene had progressed rapidly and she was sent directly to Oakland to have her leg amputated. She recovered and the Southern Sierra Power Company gave her a lifetime job on the switchboard.

The Power Company sent letters of appreciation and money to those who had helped.

Services were held near the Fred Mattly ranch for the seven whose lives had been snuffed out. Neighboring women sang songs fitting the occasion. It was clear and cold as their voices rose over the frosty Sierra.

Chapter 7

Boyhood at Mono Lake

In early May 1911, my mother and I boarded the stage for Mono Lake. I had heard interesting stories about "cowboys" and could hardly wait to see one.

As we pulled into Hector Station, I got my wish! There, astride a horse, was a young lad outfitted with chaps and a large Stetson. He pushed the hat cockily to the side of his head and said, "Hello, I am Richie Conway." Bashfully, I introduced myself.

After I had learned to ride, Richie, a Paiute friend named Sim Lundy, and I, rode together many times. People would smile and call out, "Here come the buckaroos," making the three of us feel very important. When Sim was 14 or 15 years old he had an unfortunate accident. One day as he approached Conway Summit, a whirlwind made his horse bolt. Sim was thrown into a pile of rocks. He had been lying by the trail for two days when friends found him. They took him back home, but he never did see a doctor. His leg didn't set properly, and he was crippled after that.

Richie loved horses; and even when he was in his late eighties, he still rode. He was the Grand Marshall of the Labor Day parade at Bishop, California, in 1970.

Richie and his three sisters, Pearl, Katy, and Gladys, were among my new schoolmates. The Conways were a French-Canadian family who'd settled in the Basin. For many years we would be sharing experiences. Although Pearl and Richie have passed on, we three can still "tell it like it was," in the old days at Mono Lake. For the rest of my life, Mono Basin was to be my home.

Grandmother Mary and Uncle George were glad to see us. They told us details of the avalanche, and of the hardships the big storm had caused the ranchers.

The Filosena's big, burly Italian hired hand was credited with saving my grandmother's cattle. He had shoveled several days, a distance of a third of a mile, to drive them to water.

Famous Mono "cowpoke," Richie Conway.

Sim Lundy, Paiute friend.

Young cowgirl, Katy Conway (Bell).

My mother went on to Barstow to work as a waitress at the Harvey House, where she remained for many years. I continued to live with my grandmother and uncle on the Filosena ranch.

On arrival, I was in poor health, due to my fondness for soda pop and licorice. Here I was fed good, wholesome food, and after two years I was strong enough to keep up with the other boys.

Richie Conway as Grand Marshall of Labor Day Parade, Bishop, 1970.

My uncle taught me mountain lore, and he showed me how to fish, ride horses, wrangle cows, shoot game, and help out on the ranch. These skills were necessary to survive the hardships of the coming years. They were a basic part of my education, like learning about the changing weather patterns in the Basin.

In summer, our family enjoyed many good times, one of which was the annual Fourth of July celebration at Bridgeport.[1] We were happy to visit with friends and neighbors from far and near, some we had not seen since the year before. All brought large picnic baskets, and nobody "ate out." There were the usual events, including foot races. Joe Scanavino, who was *really* a live wire, won the sack race event and foot races for

---

[1] *Bridgeport:* The original name was "Big Meadows." A footbridge crossed the town proper. When the river swelled, as it often did in the spring, the whole town would be flooded. A large bridge was eventually built at the north end of town to alleviate this condition.

many years. In the bareback rides, top honors invariably were taken by two Paiutes, Jimson and Harry Tom.

Topping off the day, was the "Grand Ball" held only on the Fourth of July and in November) and the usual fireworks, which lit up the sky with spectacular displays and loud explosions that skittered the horses.

One unusual Fourth of July, two feet of snow fell, bringing the festivities to a soggy halt, causing many folks to stay over two or three days until the roads were passable. (By the way, folks are still enjoying the yearly celebrations at Bridgeport.)

My Uncle George and I practiced our own yearly ritual before we left for Bridgeport. We rode our horses down to Mono Lake, discarded our long winter underwear, and went "skinny dipping." Only then, had summer officially arrived.

Paiute Friends

The first school was just north of Mono Inn. Lulu Biggs was one of the first teachers. Later, Lulu married the miner Phil Lorendo of Rattlesnake Gulch (to the left of Mono Diggings.)

Teacher Lulu Biggs (left) and (Mrs. Conway.

Mono Lake School.

I went to school with the Conways, De Chambeaus, and many Paiute children.

The Paiute camp was about a mile to the north of my home. As I visited the Paiute camp often, I observed their way of life, and saw the foods they ate and how they were prepared. Their diet was varied, on a "catch as catch can" basis. The grey squirrels were plentiful, as were ground hogs and sage hen, which were snared or shot. These were used in stews and soups, as a change from the abundant trout. Fishing was "out of this world" in the early days. There were fine-eating cut-throat trout in the lakes, native brook trout in the streams, and golden trout in the lakes at higher elevations. Surprisingly enough, there were few deer on the eastern slope of the Sierras; however, rabbits were plentiful, especially cottontail and jacks.

Each fall, the Paiutes looked forward anxiously to the harvesting of the pinenut crop (the nut of the piñon tree) which was very unpredictable. Whites never gathered them, so the Paiutes traded pinenuts for a similar weight of white flour. Today, they are gathered by all, selling in markets for $2.50–$4.00 per pound. Gathering them is a pitchy job, and very hard work. A long, slim pole was used by the Paiutes to knock them gently down out of the cones. The whole village would camp on the most plentiful sites, staying as long as five weeks. The Paiute women gathered the nuts, while the braves sat around making bird points (arrowheads) out of the local obsidian. Later, they would kill birds and rabbits with the points.

The nuts were stored near the "wikiups," the Paiute huts. A rock circle foundation was made, the nuts piled high within, then covered with branches and dirt to serve as insulation during the winter. They were the main source of food during the long winter ahead. The women ground them into flour for mush, bread, and soup.

Pinenuts are excellent roasted, and are very high in protein. The nuts were traded to the Diggers and Yokuts of Yosemite[2] in exchange for acorns which could be ground into a fine powder to make a mush. This was made in large quantities, and kept near or under the table. It was served cold. I had the dubious pleasure of tasting it when Nellie Reynolds, a Paiute basketmaker, offered me some, saying, "It tastes just like ice cream." We dipped our fingers in it and ate in that fashion. It was white like ice cream, but there the resemblance ended. It was *very, very* bitter.

The Mono Basin Indian (Ku-zed-i-ka Paiute) also harvested *ku-cha-bee*

---

[2] *Yosemite:* "Grizzly Bear"

Nellie Reynolds, well-known basketmaker.

from the shores of Mono Lake.[3] They were seined, then dried and added to soups or pinenut flour. In the spring, after a high protein diet of pinenuts and *ku-cha-bee*, the Paiutes eagerly gathered wild onion, wild seeds, and watercress.

They anxiously awaited the ripening of the "buckberries," in August. These grew on trees 10–16 feet tall. As far as I can determine, buckberries are native only to Mono Basin. A large grove was located along the banks of lower Rush Creek. The berries were red, tart, and juicy, resembling currants. They were gathered by placing a canvas on the ground, then hitting the branches sharply with a pole. The reasons for gathering them in this fashion, were because it was faster than "hand-picking" and because of the sharp, two-inch thorns that covered the limbs of the trees. The harvest for the day usually filled a large wash tub (5–10 gallons). Water from the creek was poured on to cover, floating off the leaves and

---

[3] Kuzedika Paiute: Before the white man came, there were nomadic hunters, gatherers, and traders living along the shores of Mono Lake. These were the Ku-zed-i-ka Paiutes, the "fly pupae" eaters. At the end of each summer, they harvested *ku-cha-bee*, the dried larvae and pupae of the Mono Lake brine flies, an important food staple. The word "Mono" means "brine fly" and "fly people," not in the Paiute language, but in the language of their Yokut neighbors, who lived in the Yosemite region and who also considered the brine fly a delicacy.

insects, leaving the fruit ready to eat. (Paiutes usually held the berries in their hand, salted them, and ate them raw. Whites simmered them for their juice, making a delicious red-orange, tangy jelly which was considered an excellent accompaniment for meat and fowl.)

Now, however, buckberry gathering is only a fond memory. The diversion of water away from Rush Creek, over a period of many years, caused the buckberry groves to wither and die. There are a few on the

Caseuse Mike.

north shore of Mono Lake that occasionally still bear small amounts of fruit.

One of the boys who lived at the camp near my home was Caseuse Mike, He and I became friends of long standing. He was very intelligent and an excellent athlete. When he was fairly young Caseuse married

Minnie Turner. Minner and her sister, Carrie Bethel, are remembered as two of the best basket makers of Mono Basin. They were responsible for numerous willow and beaded baskets, intricately patterned and finely

Prize basketmakers: Sisters Minnie Mike (left) and Carrie Bethyl.

woven. Some of their work may be seen in local museums. Although they have died, a grandson, Raymond Andrews, carries on the family crafts.

Quite often you could see Indian women gathering willow material in the vicinity of the Thompson Ranch. The willow bark was wound into coils, as twine. Other materials were used for the colored design, which usually depicted something close to nature, like the sun, coyote, rain, lighting, or snake. The red root that was used to make the dye was gathered in Yosemite.

The mothers made beautiful willow cradleboards, or *hu-ba.* These were tied together with buckskin, and had an overhang to keep the sun off the baby's face. The overhang had either a red or blue design, designating whether the baby was a girl or boy. Some cradleboards were beautifully beaded.

Paiute mothers carried their babies on their back for hours. A Paiute baby was seldom heard to cry. Paiute women worked in season on the white man's farms, leaning the baby up against a tree while they beat peas, wheat, or whatever crop they were working on against a large canvas with beaters they had made, then cleaning the seeds with winnowing baskets.

Paiute men were hired in the hay fields and did other regular farm work. When they had time, they hunted rabbits. It is a sad, but true, fact that many white employers took advantage of them. The Paiutes knew this, but were helpless to do anything about it.

As young men, Caseuse and I ran about 12 miles to and from our road jobs at Tioga Pass. We were also on the Mono Lake baseball team. Dick Charlie was our great pitcher and Harry Bethel was the catcher.

Harry Tom had a reputation as a great bronco rider. He was a small man with lots of strength and courage. At rodeos in Yosemite Valley, he often took first prize. He is well remembered for successfully riding the outlaw horse, "Steamboat."

On the south side of Mono Lake, we had no black-tail rabbits. There were cottontail and snowshoes (white), which were never very plentiful. They were prized by Paiutes and whites for their fine eating quality. At Black Point, near the north shore of Mono, there were literally thousands of black-tail jacks. The Paiutes used them as one of their main foods, relying on their skins to make warm rabbit blankets. Since it took numerous skins to make a blanket, the braves frequently had rabbit drives, most of which were at Black Point.

The method of trapping the rabbits was to weave a mesh fence 20 or 30 feet wide, and place it at the bottom of the small canyon. Two braves held the corners. Many other converged at the top and sides of the draw, carrying clubs, while herding the rabbits down into the net.

Because of the milder climate there, the Piautes usually wintered on the east side of Mono Lake, near Warm Springs. In the spring, they returned to Mono's shores to begin their food gathering.

The Paiutes loved the balmy summers. On Sundays, especially, they could be seen walking for many miles,[4] trudging to Hammond's Store to make their weekly purchases, to visit, and play the hand game (a game of chance) they enjoyed so much.

In those years at Mono Lake, I got to know many Paiutes well. I was their friend, and they were mine. Not many white men made such friendships. Most gave the Indian a bad time at every opportunity. Jake Gilbert's story is a good example.

Jake Gilbert lived at Paiute camp about six miles from the south shore of Mono Lake. He was known throughout the valley as a good worker, and excellent at breaking saddle horses. No one had ever seen Jake get bucked off by a horse. Many ranchers hired him because he could do so many things well.

In 1899, he had patiently tried to right a wrong done against him. It turned into a disaster and he got into serious trouble with the law. When I got acquainted with him, around 1914 or so, he never mentioned the episode. We often hunted rabbits and went on rabbit drives together; but what I know about the events at Samman Springs did not come from Jake.

---

[4] You could tell the Paiute families for many miles away, as they walked according to a caste system. The father walked in front; the mother or grandmother walked behind at a discrete distance; and the children were strung out in single file.

Mono County Courthouse.

 # Chapter 8

Vengeance at
Samman Springs

Old-timers will recall the ranch at Samman Springs (now known as Simmon Springs) on the south shore of Mono Lake as a hunter's paradise for geese and ducks.

I often went hunting there with my dad. We'd bring back gunny sacks of Canadian honkers, mallards, sprigs, and other birds. For several days afterward, we'd pick and prepare the fowl. Then my grandmother would place the game in large pewter crocks amid layers of salt. This preserved them perfectly and made many a delicious feast for the cold winter.

The trip took all day on a primitive road. Sometimes we didn't get home until after ten at night, when we would find Grandmother Mary anxiously waiting for us. She was relieved to see the glimmer of our headlights approaching in the distance. Once or twice, in fact, we got stuck in the deep sand all night. It took a super-human effort to grub sagebrush to place under the car wheels, as well as endless shoveling before we could resume our homeward trek.

The man who homesteaded the ranch was Louis Samman, originally from Hanford, England.[1] In 1851 he came into Yosemite as a hunter. He arrived in Dogtown in 1856, and mined there with Cord Norst and Leroy Vining. Later, he mined at Monoville, moving on to the Bodie mines about 1860.

Samman's strange attitudes and adventures indirectly led to his death at Jake Gilbert's hands in 1889. Louis Samman was once quoted by Bodie and Austin newspapers as saying he had put three Paiutes into Mono Lake to *petrify* (for scientific purposes). But, he declared, they had *putrefied*. The story was believed to be a hoax, but some people began referring to Mono Lake as "Samman's graveyard."

Louis Samman left Bodie and started his ranch near the springs. He raised cattle, pigs, and horses; and due to his reputation as a "badman," he was looked upon with suspicion by his neighbors, and with distrust and hatred by the Paiutes. This is the way my grandparents told me the story of Louis Sammon.

An understandably happy me.   *Jake Gilbert.*

[6]*Mono Diggings,* by Frank S. Wedertz, Chalfant Press, Inc., California, 1978.

"Old Samman," as he was referred to, was only seen two or three times a year when he came to buy supplies at the Hammond store. He had a gruff, swaggering manner, and toted a large six-shooter on his hip.

Meanwhile, living at the Paiute camp about six miles from the west shore of Mono Lake, near the Filosena ranch, was Jake Gilbert.

One summer, Samman hired Jake to work for him. Jake worked for him for several months, and it was said that he was beaten at times. Whenever Jake would ask for his money, Old Samman would give him a couple of dollars. That autumn, when the work was completed, Jake again asked Samman for his money. Samman gave him a few dollars, saying that was all he had coming. Jake knew better, of course, and they had a heated argument which ended with Old Samman ordering Jake off the ranch.

Often that winter Mono Lake folks got used to seeing Jake on his horse, riding out toward the Samman ranch. "My wife and children need food," Jake would say, "I'm going to see if Samman will pay me."

A story was circulating: Jake had demanded his money, Old Samman had pulled his pistol and ordered him off the ranch. Naturally, Jake was getting madder and madder at this treatment.

One day at the store, Jack Hammond told Old Samman that the Paiutes were very upset about his not paying Jake. Samman got very excited and declared he would shoot Jake if he ever caught him at his ranch again.

"It's none of my business," Jack told Samman, "but if I were you, I'd either pay Jake, or sell out and move away. The Indians are really riled up." Samman just stomped out of the store, too angry to answer.

Jake had bought an old saddle on credit from Jack Hammond who, after a while, began pressuring him for the money. Jake explained that he would pay when Samman paid him.

Jack Hammond remarked idly, "I'd kill him if I were you!"

"Yes, I kill him some day," said Jake.

Jake knew Old Samman's habits, like when he fed his hogs each evening.

One winter day, Jake took his gun and waited behind a large sagebrush until Samman came out to feed his hogs. Jake confronted him and demanded his money. Samman tried for his gun and Jake shot him in the chest, but he was not dead. Jake walked over and removed Samman's gun belt, laying it with his gun some distance away. Then Jake rode the ten miles over to Jack Hammond's saloon.

Hammond was just about to close for the night when he and a group playing poker noticed Jake standing in the doorway. He had war paint on his face and a big feather in his hair. His unusual appearance and his presence in the saloon so late at night stirred Jack's curiosity. He asked Jake how he happened to be there. Jake answered matter-of-factly:

"I shoot Old Samman. He no pay me, so I shoot him." With this, Jake rode off into the night.

Indians were hated by most whites in the West in those days; and although Old Samman was disliked by the ranchers, still they wouldn't put up with an Indian shooting a white man.

After some discussion the men rode out to Samman's place. By the time they arrived it was daylight. They found Samman lying dead in front of his cabin, between the hog pen and the house. They're supposed to have buried him there, on his ranch.

The news spread fast. Soon it was all over the country that a white man had been killed by an Indian. Of course, the story got changed around some in the telling. A lot of people didn't realize that Samman had threatened to kill Jake if he continued to ask for his money. There was talk of lynching Jake. Sheriff Cody and a posse surrounded his home. He came out quietly and they took him to the Bridgeport jail for safekeeping.

In Bridgeport saloons there was more talk of lynching. But whites weren't the only ones who were angry. Indians from all over Mono and Inyo counties gathered at the jail behind the courthouse and it's likely there would have been some shooting between whites and Indians if any attempt had been made to lynch Jake.

The trial was short and snappy — with some surprises.

Fair-minded white men who knew the facts and knew Old Samman's ways were on Jake's side.

When Jake was called to the stand and asked why he had killed Samman, he answered simply:

"I kill Samman because he no pay me my money."

"How do you know he didn't pay you all he owed you?" he was asked. (Samman, after all, had doled out a couple of bucks now and then to Jake.)

Jake asked for a pocket knife, and he started cutting notches into a railing at the witness stand. Someone quickly supplied a wooden ruler for him to use. Jake cut notches on one side to show the number of days he had worked for Samman. On the other side of the ruler, he cut a notch for each dollar paid him.

"Me know this way," Jake explained. "Me put marks on the post at ranch. I take you to ranch, show you marks on post!"

This information had a lot of bearing on the case. Because of the long distance to the ranch, the jury took Jake's word. Judge Parker gave him ten years in jail.

At this point some people started hollering about lynching, and the Indians in the courtroom looked to their guns again. The judge quieted them down, telling them:

"We are not Indians, and the Indians are not whites. But Indians as well as whites here in the county have their rights."

Most people were satisfied with the ten-year sentence, thinking it the same as a death sentence. It was said that an Indian could not live very long locked up in jail.

Jake fooled them all, though. He returned to Mono Lake after nine years at Folsom quarrying rocks, with one year off for good behavior. While he was in jail he learned to read and write and also learned blacksmithing.

I was about 15 years old when I met Jake. We became fast friends. He was a happy-go-lucky, good person to be with. Jake treasured the simple things in life — mainly his family, horses, hunting, and especially his freedom.

Like I said, he never mentioned Louis Samman, nor did I.

 # Chapter 9

Scookum and the Horse Thief

Uncle George bought me a beautiful sorrel horse from the Conway ranch at Mono Lake for $20.00. That was a lot of money in those days.

It was my first horse, and I loved him more than any horse I've ever had. Indians had captured him wild, back of Mono Lake at Whisky Flats, and he was only partly broke when I got him. I called him Scookum from a character in the funny papers. He was a good horse and carried me very far when I was young.

Scookum taught me to ride. Every morning he would buck me off. In time I got so he couldn't throw me, though it was a long while before he stopped bucking.

In 1913, when I'd had Scookum for two years, I rode him to the mining camp at Aurora, Nevada. I went to see my Aunt Mary and her husband, Uncle Frank Donnelly. Uncle Frank was working at the Magnum Mill, and I was hoping to get a job there.

They didn't hire me at the mill, so I stopped by to see Al Taylor, who ran a livery stable. Earlier, when working at the May Lundy mine, he and my Uncle George had become friends. Mr. Taylor was a very nice fellow, except when he was "in his cups," which was often.

I asked him for a job but he put me off, saying he would think it over. I hung around for several hours and finally he told me:

"I have a four-horse whip back of the stable hanging where I always keep it — on two pegs on the stable wall. Will you get it for me? I want to put a new buckskin tip on it."

I brought the whip and Mr. Taylor said he would show me how to put the tip on it; but I later learned that he had another reason for doing this. After the tip was on, he leaned the whip against the wall but kept on talking to me. Finally, he stood up and said he had to get busy. I picked up the whip and put it back in the exact same place and position on the wall.

As I started to leave, Mr. Taylor said: "Hey, George, it's about lunch time. Come home with me and have lunch. By the way, you get the job."

At lunch, he said to his wife: "I gave George a little test and he came out all right. George picked up my whip and took it back to its place without me telling him to do so; that's enough for me. I think he'll do just fine for us. I was about 14 years old at the time.

In those days there were many men roaming the country, carrying their bedroll and belongings with them. They were called tramps, or hobos. At harvest time they'd go to ranches looking for work or a handout. Ranchers would always feed them, but before hiring them they would give them the "water-test." While the food was being prepared, the hobo would be asked to fetch a bucket or two of water, either from a ditch or a well. The rancher and his wife would watch to see how the man would walk, whether slouching along, or quick and business-like. If he was quick about his business, he got the job. The water test was an established one and easy to use, becaue there was no running water in the homes at that time.

For the work at the stable I got a $1.00 a day, meals at the house, and feed for Scookum. I slept in the manger so I could guard the horses. I also fed the stock, milked the cows and delivered the milk, along with other chores. At the end of the day I was always tired and slept soundly. Mr. Taylor was a very moody man, and he and I didn't get along too well.

After about three months I woke up one morning to find that Scookum, who was stabled a little distance from where I slept, was *gone!* I ran to the Taylors. Mr. Taylor had been in his cups the night before, and

---

[1] *In his cups:* a term used at that time to denote drunkenness.

Mary (Filosena) Donnelly, husband Frank, and children Doris, Clifford, and Florence.

was very cranky, but his wife talked him into letting me have a saddle horse to go look for Scookum, whom we all realized had been stolen.

Finding a stolen horse was difficult. I had spent all my wages the day before and Mr. Taylor wouldn't advance me any, moralizing that if I had saved my money I wouldn't be broke. Mrs. Taylor wanted to help me but he wouldn't let her, so I saddled the horse and started out. It was now late in the day.

I didn't know which way to go. Bodie seemed as good a bet as any, so I headed south. Along the way, I asked everybody I met if they had seen Scookum.

Halfway to Bodie, I saw two men on horseback coming toward me. They had big pistols in their gun belts and looked like pretty hard cases; but they were friendly enough and asked me where I was going. I told them about my stolen horse, told them that Scookum was a sorrel with a dark mane and a worn saddle, and told them how big he was. Sure

concluded, "Now, come with me back to Wellington so you can verify my story and be on your way with your horse."

I told him I believed his story, especially as the big man had been seen earlier riding my horse back Bodie way. I was so happy to see Scookum back, and we decided to ride on to Aurora together. We laughed and became quite friendly, and he told me he was from Oklahoma. It was very late when we came upon a farm where there was a place for teamsters and travelers to eat.

We stabled our horses in the large barn nearby. My friend paid for supper and feed for our horses, and we slept in the hay loft.

Next morning, I could hear the teamsters getting up; but it was still dark and I was exhausted, so I slept on. When I finally did get up, all the teamsters had gone — and to my suprise, so had my friend.

I checked the corral, and saw that Scookum was still there. I relaxed and went to find the owner of the ranch. He told me that the teamsters' flunky had bit the bottle the night before and was sleeping it off behind the big sagebrush. My friend, knowing the freighter was shorthanded, got a job on the spot and was heading for Minden with the teamsters.

The rancher and his wife invited me to breakfast, but I told them I had no money. That was all right, the wife said: I was not expected to pay. I ate and thanked them, got my horses, and headed for Aurora, arriving tired and hungry at dusk. Mr. Taylor was still in his cups, and in a bad mood. He started right in on me again for not noticing the thief before Scookum was taken, and he was probably right. But this time I was tired of haggling about the whole darn thing, so I left Mr. Taylor early the next morning and headed back for Mono Lake.

Scotty John and the Black Stallion

I left at daylight, expecting to get to my Grandmother Filosena's ranch at Mono Lake early in the day, but I hadn't counted on meeting up with wild horses and a not-so-wild Indian. As I was riding by the Paiute camp near Aurora, I caught up with an Indian whom I knew real well.

Scotty John was planning to run some wild horses back of Mono Lake. He had his eye on a beautiful stallion in the bunch, which he'd chased before and wanted real bad. A cowboy in Aurora had told him that if he could crease the stallion, it would be easier to catch him. Scotty carried a .22 rifle. He was going to try this and wanted me to help.

We took a short cut through the mountains to Mono Lake and made camp at the Whisky Flats area, where we saw several bands of wild horses. Our only food was a piece of Indian bread that Scotty had stowed away in a little bag. Next morning, we were off at early daylight to see which band of horses had the black stallion for leader. My eyes were good in those days, but not so good as Scotty's. He spotted the stallion with a small band headed for the fresh water springs some distance away.

Scotty told me to take the bridle and saddle off Scookum, and he did the same with his horse. We left the ropes around our horses' necks. By bending low and leading them on foot, we got quite close to the band before they became aware of us. Scotty's plan was to have the black stallion see our horses, get curious about whether they were mares, and come close before catching our scent.

It worked: the beautiful black horse circled us, coming closer and closer until Scotty figured it would get no nearer.

Creasing the stallion went like this: Scotty was supposed to put a bullet right on the upper part of the stallion's neck, in an area no larger than three inches. The stallion was in good position and Scotty was a dead shot. He fired, and the stallion went down.

We tied our horses to sagebrush, took two ropes and ran to the downed horse. The stallion was up at once, tail flying high as he raced to his band and rushed them off across the flats toward the hills. Scotty and I mounted again and followed the band from hill to hill, trying to get close enough so Scotty could rope one of the mares. We charged, but the stallion and his mares beat us across the flats. Scotty said he knew of a corral across the flats and motioned to turn them in that direction.

As we got the band running, Scotty's horse gave out and fell. Scookum kept the pace, though, and I herded the wild horses into the corral. I counted sixteen of them, and I stood guard at the entrance so they couldn't come out.

Before Scotty could give me a hand, the black stallion had jumped over the coiled log bars at the other end of the corral. He didn't quite clear them, but he knocked enough of them down to allow the band to escape, screaming and streaking for the hills.

For now, we had to call it quits, but we vowed that we'd return again in search of the black stallion.

The two of us headed for Scotty's father's ranch, many miles away.

Scotty had to walk a lot, his horse was so done in. It was late in the afternoon when we arrived at the Paiute camp. Captain John invited me in for pinenut soup, but I wasn't hungry. Scotty and I had stopped to buy cheese and bread at the Petrie ranch some miles back.

After a while, I took my leave and continued on to my Grandmother Mary's ranch at Mono Lake.

This time I made it, and slept soundly in my own bed at last.

 # Chapter 10

Goat Hunting on Paoha

For several months I helped out at the ranch. Fall turned into winter. One cold winter morning I had a disagreement with Pete Roberts. In a huff, I rolled up my bedroll and walked the mile and a half to the lake shore to bunk with an Austrian friend, Dan Guis, who had a cabin there.

A few days later a horseman brought a message that my friend John Bellye, the blacksmith at Hammond's, wanted to see me. I was about 14 at the time and John was about 50, but we enjoyed each other's company. He had been a fisherman in San Francisco before coming to Mono Lake. He was a very good mechanic and knew a lot about repairing engines. I ran most of the way from Mono Inn to Hammond's to see him.

I arrived breathless to find John, a heavy drinker, in high spirits. He had fixed up the very boat that had belonged to the unlucky Mr. Nay, and he wanted me to shoot wild goats with him on Paoha Island.

Fresh meat sounded like a good idea, so I went down to the lake shore to help him untie the boat. The weather was cloudy and the lake was rough. I timidly mentioned this, but John put me off by telling me a long story about how he'd fished in high seas off San Francisco, and that "this little pond" couldn't trouble him or his boat. (Mono was about 90 square miles of surface then, but it was a "little pond" to John Bellye that winter morning.)

We put our guns in the boat. I had a .30-.30 rifle. John had a .38 pistol and a rifle. I was a dead shot with my rifle, and had won money on Sundays at Mono Lake shooting meets. So, in spite of the weather, I was feeling great as we started out, and so was John.

About halfway across the lake the motor died. It took us an hour to start it up again. The wind was blowing hard by the time we reached Paoha Island and tied up the boat in a little bay on the east side.

The white island, Paoha, is about three miles long and a half-mile wide. We'd walked a mile when we found several bands of goats. Two bands ran away; but one ewe with four little kids had to stay. There were also a big buck and four she-goats. John wanted to do most of the shooting, but he was a poor shot. I got one she-goat then and there, and one more as she was going over a hill. The buck got away. Not to be outdone,

Paoha goat: imported Swiss Toggenburg buck "Prince Bismark," 203 lbs.

John shot the nursing ewe. The four kids ran around in a circle crying for their mother (and I wasn't too pleased at the sight). Before I could stop him, John had pulled his pistol and shot all four of the kids. The boat was some distance away, and we had to move it about a mile up the shore to put the goats in. By this time it was late in the afternoon and the weather was turning nasty.

We put the goats in the front of the boat, which made it full. We had three she-goats and one kid on top. It was hard getting the boat far enough out from shore to get it started, and by the time we made it, the waves were fairly high.

Then it started to snow.

I yelled at John to tie the boat up, and that we should stay overnight, or at least until the storm died down. But this only made him angry. I knew I should stay behind and let him try to get back by himself, but there was no wood and I had no food. Under the circumstances, there was nothing to do but go along with him.

Right away we began to have trouble. A mile or so from shore, the engine died and we almost drifted back onto the island. The trouble, so John said, was with the magneto or carburetor. We made some adjustments and started out again.

We were about two miles out when the engine quit again. I'd gotten out the spare oars and was trying to keep the boat from going sideways in the rough gale that was getting worse by the minute. We drifted close to the island again, but I didn't even suggest trying to land in that storm. We would have had to leave the boat and swim to shore, and would certainly have frozen to death, given the temperature of Mono Lake in winter.

Again, we reached the middle of the lake. The storm was really on us now and it was snowing hard. The boat was nose-heavy with the weight of the goats, and the spray from the waves butting the front was awful. Freezing cold water was splashing our engine; and, of course, we were soaking wet, even though we were well-dressed and had good gloves. This time, maybe it was the spray from the waves that stopped the engine. Anyway, stop it did. John had me on the oars trying to keep the boat straight. He had pulled off his gloves to work on the boat and his hands were freezing. Even with gloves on, my hands felt like ice.

It was almost dark. The front end of the boat was digging into the waves so much that John threw the top goat into the lake to lighten the load. He would have thrown out more of them, but his hands were so cold he couldn't get enough of a grip to pull them out. He went back to the engine, which was now soaking wet, and started to crank it. But his icy hands could no longer hold the crank.

His hand wasn't too cold to hold onto a bottle, however. He dragged a half-filled whisky bottle from his pack, opening it with his teeth. He had the bottle up to his mouth for some time, then passed it to me. I couldn't let go of the oars to take any. John put the bottle down, got on his knees, looked up toward the unseen sky and, to my horror, started *praying!*

Up to this time, I'd had great confidence in John, but when I saw this I gave up all hope. "Two more men will be drowned in Mono Lake," I thought. The oars were slipping through my frozen hands. The boat was tossing wildly in the wind, jumping high in the waves, out of control. John was lying over the engine of the boat, not moving. Water was getting deeper and deeper in the boat. I decided to crank the engine one more time. Lo and behold! It started! At once, John came out of his stupor.

The engine wasn't running right and threatened to stop; John worked under the cover of his sheepskin coat, and finally got it going.

Yes, John was a good mechanic; he knew engines. His face began to take on new life. We had a hard time of it; and at times, even with the engine at full power, we were standing still. But in the dark we made it to shore. There were no waves at Hammond's, where we landed, and the storm was dying down. We helped each other out of the boat and, through two feet of new snow, we stumbled to John's cabin, almost frozen. It was hard to get a fire started in the wood stove, with our hands still numb. John had another bottle of whisky in his cabin. This time both of us took long swigs. Later, we heated water and had hot whisky drinks. We took off our clothes to dry ourselves by the wood stove. Both of us got the shakes so bad our teeth were clicking. The shakes lasted until almost morning, when we finally got to sleep. We slept all that day and all the following night.

The storm was over, and weather real nice again. The next day, after our day-and-night sleep, we went down to the boat and finally, after a lot of pulling, we got all the frozen goats out. We carried them up to a big tree by John's cabin and laid them on the ground.

John said, "Georgie, you have a skinning job to do now." (John had never skinned an animal in his life.)

"John," I told him, "I don't have any skinning job to do. I am not going to skin those goats. Furthermore, I don't want any of the meat. I am finished with the whole goat deal. I am going home." And that is exactly what I did, with John cursing me until I was out of hearing distance, and probably farther.

I found out later that John had gotten Jansen, an Indian lad, to skin the goats in return for one of them, plus some whisky. John offered me some of the meat later, but I didn't want any. He asked me not to tell anyone what a bad time we'd had on Mono Lake. He had a lot of pride, and didn't want to chance losing face.

"*Now* do you believe that Mono Lake is dangerous?" I asked him.

He answered, "Georgie, for a little lake, it's worse than the ocean."

John went back to San Francisco and I never saw or heard from him again. The boat lay abandoned around the shore for several years. I wasn't a bit sorry when waves finally broke it up.

Chapter 11

Trapping at Tioga

That same, eventful year of 1913, I put in a winter trapping with my two best friends, George Joos and Evert Mattly. Our camp was a bunkhouse built by the Southern Sierra Power Company for a dam they had planned. It was about three miles from Tioga summit, at about 9500 feet at Rhinedollar Lake (now known as Ellery Lake). The bunkhouse was large, with a big kitchen, plenty big enough for four men. The fourth member of our trapping team was an Italian called Long John. He was the oldest of our group, and had been a miner and a gambler. My friends were at least ten years older than I. Long John was tall, with a dark complexion, on the thin side and as hard a worker as I have ever seen. He'd managed to lose all his money gambling. He had never trapped before, but he was willing to try, albeit reluctantly.

We all laid out our traps: Evert and I took the south side of Rhinedollar Lake as far as Mt. Dana, up to the summit and around the old Tioga Mine district, near the Sheepherder Mine. Long John had his lines near camp. George had the longest line, his area extending to Saddlebag. We were trapping for marten and fox, as well as cross fox (a mixed breed). There was a great demand for silver fox, and silvers had been seen at Tioga through the years. George had high hopes for trapping the valuable silver fox.

Our winter food supply was laid in, and when we wanted mail or other items, we'd ski the 3000 feet from Tioga Pass down to Hammond's at Mono Lake, a full day's trip each way. Long John never made these trips because he hated to use snowshoes or skis.

For a time all went well at camp; but then big snows came and outside of laying and checking the trap lines, there was nothing to do. The trapping was poor and we began to get on each other's nerves. George Joos and I had made a bargain at the beginning, that we'd be partners in any furs we caught; and one day, as I met him on the trap line, he said, "Georgie, let's split the camp; I don't like the way things are going."

George Joos and unknown boy.

I said I'd like to split, but how? He said there was an old cabin up at the Tioga mine that could be turned into a camp for the two of us, even though it was in bad shape. I asked how we would cook, since there was neither stove nor bed in the cabin. George said he had seen a small stove in one of the cabins by Rhinedollar Lake; That day we stopped by one of the cabins to look things over. Cooking utensils were scattered all over and there was an old bed — and, yes, a stove. A very *heavy,* cast-iron stove.

"George," I said, "We can't carry that stove three miles on snowshoes to the cabin at Tioga.

"Don't let the weight of the stove worry you," replied George. "If we take off all the loose hardware, I can carry it on my back."

I knew that George was stronger than any of us; on our trips up from Mono Lake, George carried more pounds than either Evert or I could, and he always broke trail as well. Still, I worried.

There was a big pow-wow when George announced our plans to Evert and Long John; but we finally convinced them that we needed our *own* camp so we could get an earlier start in the mornings. The next morning, George and I started carrying out our gear. I thought we ought to get the stove hauled first, because if we couldn't manage to get the stove there, we'd have to haul our belongings back — over three miles of deep snow!

"I told you, Georgie," said my pal George Joos, "that *I* would take care of the stove. When we're ready, I'll move it. All I want you to do is break trail for me when the time comes."

Up at Tioga we prepared our traps, got a woodpile ready, and began fixing the cabin. Knowing we'd need fresh meat, we skied down to the Chris Mattly ranch at Lee Vining Creek (about the same distance as to Hammond's), and brought back half of a hog, hanging it on a pine tree at our new camp. It froze quickly. Whenever we wanted meat, we'd chop off what we needed with an axe.

Finally, everything was moved in except the stove. Evert and Long John offered to help. It took the three of us to lift it. George tied a rope around it, got on his knees, and we arranged the stove on his back. We broke trail ahead of him and had to re-arrange the stove each time he stopped to rest. Finally, just minutes before a winter storm hit, we got the stove into the cabin.

The big storm hit so suddenly, as storms frequently do in the area, that Evert and Long John couldn't leave. The four of us stayed all night in that little one-room cabin at Tioga. None of us slept very much; we put in our time melting snow in a five-gallon can and getting more wood for the fire. We covered the chinks and cracks to keep the cabin snug, and drank lots of coffee that night.

Water was a real problem in winter. Usually, snow was melted in large cans on the stove. However, snow water by itself will put a human being in bad condition quickly, so we always put pieces of square nails in the water for 12 hours or more until the iron in the nails started to work in the snow water. At no time did you want to be without a pot of beans. They were a must; and we'd put iron in the water when we soaked them overnight. At such high altitudes a little baking soda helped the beans cook faster. If the beans went sour, we would re-boil them, because sour beans make a person very sick.

The next morning, after a breakfast of flapjacks and molasses, we set the beans on the fire to cook with big pieces of pork. After we finished them off, Evert and John left.

That was a cold, mean winter. Since I was younger and not as strong as George, he always did more than his share. He always had kindling ready to light. He'd get up first, light the stove, and jump back into bed until the place heated up. We ate on tin plates, setting them down on top of the stove while we were eating to keep the food from getting too cold.

The trapping was very poor indeed that winter. Lots of work and hardship for practically nothing; but we lived on hopes of getting a silver fox. Fox tracks appeared from time to time, but somehow the foxes themselves avoided our traps. Then, a really big snow hit the Sierras; about 15 feet of snow on the level. The landscape changed so much that we could not locate our traps. John fared the worst of us all. He lost almost all of his traps. Evert and I lost about half of ours. George, a true woodsman, never lost a trap at any time.

One day, Evert told George that he and John had caught a beautiful cross fox and had him in the spare room at the bunkhouse. We went to see him. He was large and beautiful. At first, he wouldn't eat or drink; he jumped around a lot. In about a week he began to eat a little, and finally tamed down a bit. Evert and John wanted to catch another one — they thought they might start a fox farm from a pair. I met Evert going to his camp one day with a barley sack in his arms. In it was another cross fox he had just caught. He had tied its legs; but when he opened the sack to show it to me, the fox was dead. It had died of fright.

Before the end of the trapping season, John and Evert had shot another cross fox. They hated to do this but its pelt brought them $44.00. Those were the only two animals Evert and John caught the entire winter.

George and I fared a little better. We trapped 28 marten, which we sold to Earl Patterson for $1.00 apiece, and two bobcat for $40.00 apiece. (Nowadays bobcat furs sell for $225.00, and many are shipped to Italy.) George and I had seen three cross foxes, but we missed the big one, the silver.

We had set out a horse's head for bait at a trap not far from our cabin. One morning, George found that a fox had been eating it, but the traps had frozen and so didn't work. The same thing happened a few days later. This time, we placed some bacon strips along with the horse's head for bait.

About a week went by. One morning George woke me up, very excited.

"Get up," he said. "We have a silver fox in the traps!"

I got up in a hell of a hurry; George was already out the door and running on his snowshoes. As we got near the horse's head, the silver fox turned his head, looked at us, and ran away. He hadn't been caught in the trap at all. The movements he'd been making, pulling on the horse's head as he ate, just made it seem like he was caught and was trying to escape.

We were so disppointed that we talked about it for a long time. Day and night, that's all we could think about. In those days, a large silver fox pelt sold for $1000 and up. Wages were $2 per day, so you can see what the pelt would have meant to us. In later years, there were so many fox farms in Canada and the United States, that prices for silvers fell very low and trappers had to quit this trade. But things were different when we were trapping at Tioga.

Early one morning, Evert and I started off on skis into Yosemite Park (about three miles away) to trap for marten. George stayed at camp because he was afraid to leave on an overnight trip for fear he would miss the silver. If the silver were caught, George wanted to be right there, before the fox could bite his foot off and escape.

We each had a few traps, some tree squirrels for bait, and candy bars and raisins for food. It was not a good morning, and I told Evert maybe we should wait until it looked better. He said no. He figured we'd be able to make it to Tuolomne Meadows and to the big, main Park cabin before dark. A few miles into Yosemite the weather got worse, but we kept going.

Main Park cabin, Yosemite National Park.

The storm hit us suddenly; we were buffeted by heavy winds and swirling snow. We were in a blizzard so fierce we could hardly see where we were going, and by then it was too late to turn back. We tried to follow the road, but the snow was so deep and the blizzard so violent, this was out of the question.

We headed into the wind and snow, hoping to find the cabin. Some time later, we reached what we thought was Tuolomne Meadows, but we could not be sure. We were lost and began to fear the worst. Our strength was giving out. We threw away our packs to lighten the load. This proved to be one of the worst mistakes we made during that whole nightmare of a trip.

Then, a miracle occurred; it was one chance in a thousand — Evert came upon the smokestack of the fireplace of the big Park cabin. He was shouting to me, but the wind blew his voice away. As I got closer, I saw the smoke stack sticking out of the snow. The rest of the cabin was covered. We took off our skis and started to dig down into the snow to find the door. After a very long time we found it, though by this time, because we had stopping walking, we had begun to freeze. Our mittens were wet, as was our clothing: wet and freezing. We stomped our feet and slapped our hands together. The blizzard lessened, but the snow was falling fast and darkness was not far away.

We kept digging and finally found the huge knob that opened the door; but we also found a huge padlock on it. Evert pulled a medium-sized limb off a nearby pine tree and hit the lock repeatedly. Useless. We used the limb to pry loose a small rock near the door. We struck at the lock over and over, but it would not break open. The wind had died down and we could now hear each other.

"It's hell to die now, when we've made it to the cabin," said Evert. "But if we can't get in we'll freeze right here."

"Evert," I said, "We still have a chance. I can crawl down that chimney to the fireplace."

We inspected the top of the chimney. Evert was too big for the opening, but I thought I could make it. I took off my coat and almost froze. Quickly, I climbed down into the small opening. We had cleared the snow from around the windows and found that they were covered with steel plates, but I figured that once inside we might be able to start a fire and then figure some way to get out — if we ever wanted out!

Once inside the chimney, I made my way down as far as possible, hanging on to the top with my hands. Then I let go and fell — all of 12 inches! We had not taken into account that fireplace chimneys taper toward the base. So there I was, stuck fast in a freezing chimney. Evert hollered to me and I told him I was stuck. "What a way to die," I thought, "stuck in a sooty chimney!"

In those days we all carried long pine snow poles, and now Evert dropped his down to me. I was able to climb it nearly to the top; but this was still not close enough for Evert to grab my hands. I could touch the ends of his fingers and that was all. I put the pole against the front of my chest and grabbed it with both hands. My hands were so frozen I could hardly hold on; but when death is close you'd be surprised what strength and effort you can put forth. Evert pulled, while I pushed on the rough inner sides of the chimney with my feet. Eventually, I got up far enough so he could grab my wrists and pull. I was out! I was blackened, half-frozen, and generally a mess. But I was alive! I was so cold I could hardly get my coat on again.

We were both sick and scared.

"George," Evert told me, "We'll have to move on. Now that the wind has died down some, maybe we can get to a place where we can build a fire."

I doubted we were in any shape to build a fire at all, but we had to keep moving. We tried one last time to break the lock with the rock. It was no use. While Evert put on his skis, I picked up the rock and beat the lock in frustration. Just a few blows — and the lock sprang open! I hollered as loud as I could: "We're saved!" and hit the door with my shoulder.

It didn't budge! Desperately, we rammed our shoulders against the door, over and over again. We hit it so many times we got a little warmth back into our bodies. We knew we might still die, right in front of that frozen door. It was enough to make a person lose his senses, and we almost did. Especially when we remembered the little hatchet tucked away in Evert's pack, which we'd discarded. That hatchet could have saved our lives. It could have opened the lock, or cut us a heavy limb to use as a battering ram.

"We have one more chance left, if we hurry," Evert told me. "It's almost dark, but if you go one way and I go another, maybe we can find a pine limb big enough to bump that door open."

With our last strength, we started out in opposite directions to find a limb. It was hard to see anything because of the falling snow and the darkness. The snow was so deep it put most limbs out of our reach, so a dry limb was our only hope. As I searched for one, I heard Evert calling my name from a long way off. I answered back, and in a short time I plowed through the snow to join him. He had found a huge, partly dead tree with a large limb that looked just right. He thought, we could break it off by bouncing up and down on it. So we bounced. Up and down, up and down; and once we thought we heard it crack. We rested and bounced again. By this time we were both nearly hysterical, thinking how our lives depended on our bouncing up and down until we broke that limb off.

The limb broke so suddenly that we were thrown into deep snow. Clambering up, we saw the break was a clean one, just what we needed. We felt lucky, for now it was quite dark and snowing heavily, and we were certain this was the only limb we were going to get.

Back in front of the door, we took hold of the limb and rammed with all our strength. Still, the door didn't budge. Again and again we rammed, until we could hardly lift the limb. After short rests, we would try again. Evert turned to me and said:

"Can you beat this? To lose our lives right at this door! Dammit, Georgie, it can't be! This door has got to open!"

We kicked out more snow to make extra room for a final rush with our ramming limb. We took a good rest, with the understanding that we'd put all of our remaining strength into just two more of the hardest rams we could manage. It worked! On the second rush, the door game way and we fell into the room, carrying with us the limb, and what seemed like half the snow in Yosemite as well.

I cannot ever describe how we felt when we finally hit the floor of that room. We felt like crying, and both of us got the shakes real bad. We later asked ourselves why we got the shakes so bad *after* the danger was over. I presume that after so much tension, our nerves just gave way when the tension was released.

We managed to get the door shut again. Inside it was cold and dark as pitch. Slapping our hands together and stomping around cautiously in the dark, we kept bumping into things we couldn't see. Evert ran into a woodpile stacked against the wall of the room. Feeling the pieces of wood, he groaned, "I sure wish I had my hatchet now." One of us felt a small sliver, then another. This I lit with a waterproof match that had belonged to Grandfather Filosena, who had used it when he worked in the May Lundy mine. The burning sliver lit up the darkness briefly. Evert saw some kindling off a way from where we were.

In darkness again, we shook so badly we had trouble doing anything. We each had a pocket knife; and when we located the kindling, I sat down with a stack of it between my knees. Because I had the biggest and best knife, I began whittling off slivers with my shaking hands. Before long, I had a little pile of whittlings, and I lit them.

Now we had light!

We'd found the fireplace, and in no time had a big fire going. There was enough wood inside the cabin to last for several days; but a strange thing kept happening to us. The warmer we got, the more we shivered. We dragged mattresses down from the loft in the cabin and lay down on them in front of the fire. Still, we shook so hard we had to get up and walk around. That was the only way we could relieve the shakes.

Late that night, Evert felt better. By daylight he was all right. I still had the shakes. We opened the door a crack to see what was going on outside, as the windows were covered with those steel plates. The wind had come up strong again and it was snowing hard, with no signs of letting up.

Suddenly we were hungry!

All we had was a few raisins left in our pockets. The food had been in those foolishly discarded packs. Were we going to starve then, in this warm room into which we'd finally won our way?

The Silver Fox

No, fate hadn't decreed that Evert and I were to die of starvation. In Yosemite Park that hungry, snowbound morning, we found food in the cabin, all we could eat. Canned goods, rice, and — wonder of wonders — coffee! We were busy that morning: getting snow melted for cooking and opening cans. We ate and ate. Then we slept for two days and two nights.

On the morning of the third day, the sun came out bright and warm; the skies were clear. We left the cabin in good shape, pulling the heavy door shut behind us and replacing the padlock. On an impulse, I picked up the rock we had used to pound the lock open. On this bright morning, I pounded on that lock with all my might and from every direction. I couldn't budge it.

"God must have been with us," said Evert. That was the only way he could figure that lock had opened for us in our desperate need. Now, I won't say this was the case; but I won't say it was not the case, either.

We got back to camp, minus our packs, but in good shape. George and John had been very worried about us, and were surprised we had survived. Gardisky, a Russian friend and an expert trapper, came by our camp and told us that trapping was poor in Yosemite. So we gave that up.

George Joos never for a minute gave up the idea that he could catch the silver fox; but his hopes died down toward spring. About the last of February, he told me one morning we ought to go to Mono Lake for fresh meat and supplies. I said I would stay and watch for the fox, but he said no.

"No need for you to stay. I'll need you to help me carry some of the supplies," he said. "Tomorrow morning, we'll check our baits and sets before we leave; then we'll go to Mono Lake and buy our supplies. We can leave early next morning and get back before it gets too late to check the traps."

I wish I had insisted on staying, anyway, but looking back doesn't help. And I really thought it would be a waste of time to sit and watch for the silver fox to come back to our traps.

We skied to Mono Lake in record time, downhill all the way. At Hammond's we bought our supplies. Chris Mattly was there by chance and we got a lift to his ranch, where we picked up fresh meat. There was always fresh meat hanging there.

Late that night the wind woke us up. In the morning it was blowing so hard it was difficult to haul hay to Chris's cattle a short way from his house. Chris and most of the farmers in those days got up at daylight. By the time we fed the cattle, the snow was coming down and the wind was blowing hard. Of course, we had to give up our trip back to the traps for the day.

Trouble was, it snowed for three days and three nights without stopping. We helped Chris with the cattle as well as shoveling the snow around his house and barns. It took a long time for the snow to settle afterward, as it was very dry. When we tried moving in it we sank way down; but George *had* to start back and that was all there was to it. Because of the silver fox, of course.

We started off right after daybreak on the fourth day. I believe the distance to our Tioga cabin was 16 miles, but of course, this time it was all uphill. We sank deeply with our skis at every step. George and I took turns breaking trail until we got to Warren Creek. There I became so exhausted that George had to take the lead. I had a hard time following his trail and by the time we reached Rhinedollar Lake I suggested that we stay over with Evert and Long John. George, however, insisted on continuing: I could stay if I wanted to. I felt I would die before giving up, so I followed his tracks while he went on ahead, out of sight. He reached the cabin quite some time before I did. It was very dark when I got there, and George had the beans already heated for me to eat.

Next morning all hell broke loose. George had gotten up extra early, anxious about the long-unattended traps. I was still eating when he came back.

"Georgie," he said, "I have some bad news. We caught the fox, and I'm sure it was the silver. Anyway, we did catch something. But both the drag and the traps have disappeared under the snow."

I told him it could have been cross foxes, or even coyotes; but there was no convincing George that he hadn't lost the silver a second time. He was sick and so was I, though I tried not to let on how bad I felt. We took our skis and long poles and poked down in the snow to see if we could feel animals under the snow pack. We poked and shoveled for several days but we could never find any drag or traps or animals. This upset George so much we broke camp and came down to Mono Lake. He went to the Mattly ranch to help Chris out, and I returned to the Filosena ranch to give Grandmother Mary a hand.

About the first of June, George told me he was going back where we'd been to see what had really happened. Maybe it would have been better if he hadn't gone. In a gully, about 50 yards from where the trap had been set, he found the drag trap on a big, beautiful male silver fox. Patches of snow in the gully, as well as the cold nights, had kept the silver in perfect condition. But as George reached for his prize, he came away with a handful of rotten fur. From being dead so long, and from lying around in the June heat, the silver's fur was useless. George checked the fur against his price list. We determined that our silver fox would have been worth twelve to fifteen hundred dollars! We'd come so close! Even caught, the silver had eluded us.

This venture marked the end of our trapping partnership. The next spring George and I headed out to Bakersfield to look for work. Both of us trapped in later years, but never together; and when Death came, tragically and prematurely for my old friend George, I guess you could say a silver fox accomplished what all the German sharpshooters failed to do. I was nowhere near when George Joos died up there on his trapline. This is how it happened:

George was still a young man in his late twenties, when he decided he wanted to get married. He corresponded with an Iowa farm girl named Effie. They became engaged in 1922, and made plans to be married in the spring of 1923. George set a trapline from Silver Lake (one of the lakes in the Grant Lake loop) over the mountain to Mammoth. On December 17, he set out for Mammoth on a fine morning, thinking to check his line and still hoping for that silver fox. There was no snow that morning, and George went without snowshoes so he could make better time. While he was at Mammoth, one of those sudden Sierra storms came up, and

George never made it back to his camp at Silver Lake. Throughout the next spring, Effie waited for his return. Their wedding date came and went, and still George did not show up.

Now, George Joos was no greenhorn when it came to snow traveling, as I have said; yet, when they found his body in late spring, it seemed, strangely enough, that he had simply sat down in the snow to smoke a cigarette, and had frozen to death right there. He was found close to his camp, in a sitting position, with his back against a large pine tree, his rifle across his legs, his pack on his back, and a can of tobacco and cigarette papers on his lap.

They buried George on the spot, with his boots on. A small lake nearby bears his name, as does the creek descending from it. The spelling of his name has been changed to *Yost.* The Forest Service maintains a brass plate attached to the tree under which he died as a tribute to a great mountain man.

HERE RESTS THE REMAINS OF

GEORGE JOOS
—TRAPPER—SOLDIER—FRIEND—

WHO DIED AS HE LIVED
FIGHTING LIKE A MAN

——————————— • ———————————

PERISHED BY THIS TREE DEC. 19, 1921 IN A BLIZZARD AFTER A 36 HOUR STRUGGLE. BORN AT VERSAN, SWITZERLAND AUG. 24, 1894. FOUND AT THIS SPOT JUNE 25, 1922. BURIED HERE JUNE 27, 1922.
                    REQUIESCAT IN PEACE

Evert Mattly, another partner in that Tioga trapping adventure met his death in a manner just as strange. He froze to death in Mono Lake many years later. The official report said "heart attack." This is what happened.

Evert was duck hunting there one winter. He shot two fine ducks that fell out in the lake. Evert, always known as a tough mountain man (and I knew it for fact), took off his clothes and started to swim out to get his ducks. Like most of us oldtimers, he had done this many times before. But this time, when Evert hit that cold lake water, his heart gave out. He was found later in the day by Larry Hess, another duck hunter, who noticed Evert's nude body bobbing up and down on the surface of the lake.

The reluctant fourth man on our Tioga trip, the miner Long John, was a gambler, as I've said before. He would save up a stake for months and then lose it all in one night.

The power company at Rhinedollar Lake gave him a big contract to blast out the side of a mountain so as to free up rock that the power company needed for making a dam on the lake. Long John and some other men drilled a tunnel into the side of the mountain. They placed a few tons of "giant" powder in the tunnel (T.N.T.), and blasted out the side. Long John got $4000.00 for this job. Right away, he went down to Hammond's and got into a poker game with a "shark" from Benton, named Jess Mount.

Now Jess Mount is a story unto himself. They say he left Benton and quit gambling because a friend of his who had lost all his money in a poker game with Jess, had gone out and killed himself. After that, Jess refused to get into a poker game with anybody. Naturally, legends began to grow up around the gambler who refused to gamble.

Long John had heard the legend and he became obsessed with getting Jess Mount to gamble with him. He took that $4000.00 and hung around Hammond's place, nagging Jess about playing poker. Jess was irritated and repeatedly told him to "find someone in your own class to play with." But this only irritated Long John. There were other poker players around Hammond's, but Long John refused to play with anyone but Jess. Finally, Jess got fed up with Long John's insults and taunts. Late one afternoon, he told John:

"Okay, so you have $4000.00. Put it on the table. I'll also put in $4000.00."

Jess always had a lot of money stashed away: nobody knew where or how much. He told John: "5-card stud poker, $5.00 ante," and John happily agreed.[1]

---

[1] John Dondero was hired to referee the game.

Jess continued: "Furthermore, when I have all your money, I don't ever want to hear you talk about gambling again!" John said that was OK.

By ten o'clock that night, Long John was clean broke; but he never cried about his loss. In fact, he seemed quite happy: he had been in a poker game with the legendary Jess Mount. Apparently that was worth $4000.00 to him.

The next day Long John was seen walking along the road toward Bodie. Later, I heard he was at Masonic, a mining town near Bridgeport. That was the last I ever heard of him.

Chapter 12

Return to Bakersfield

Just a little more than a quarter of a century earlier, my father, J.B., had arrived in Bakersfield looking for a man he had sworn to kill. In the fall of 1914, in a season of intense heat, George Joos and I decided to look for work in Bakersfield. I didn't have to go looking for work, really. I was only 15 and there was plenty of work for me to do on my grandmother's ranch. I guess I wanted to prove myself. I was looking for adventure. George was an extra strong man, a good and honest man.

When he first came to this country from Switzerland, George worked for his uncle Pete Gilli, who had a large ranch in Bakersfield. We figured we could find work with Mr. Gilli. I had met George a couple of years earlier, when he was working for another uncle, Chris Mattly. George was a milker by trade. He had big corns on his thumbs from years of milking in the old country. He was a good cook, too, and an excellent horseman.

George and I had two saddle horses: a large colt and a pack horse by the name of Banjo. We left early in the morning from Chris Mattly's ranch with high hopes and very little money. We went by way of Tioga Pass, camping the first night at Tuolomne Meadows. Early next morning, we headed for Yosemite Valley over the trail at Lake Tenaya.

As we started down into the valley, all hell broke loose. Old Banjo went wild, bucking up a storm and finally running off. All our careful packing went to pieces — pots and pans were flying every which way. The horses were totally out of control. It was then that we saw the fresh bear tracks.

We camped on the valley floor, getting there a little before dark. We weren't alone. There were other campers with large herds of mules and horses. They'd made a corral to hold all the stock, and they had hay and oats to feed them. There were also some gypsy horse traders. In those days there were lots of horse traders . . . and some horse thieves as well.

In the morning, we took the Wawona road toward Fresno, and about halfway there we met a man who looked like he might be a horse thief. He rode with us a while and then left; and that very night, thieves tried to steal our horses. I was young and couldn't stay awake too long, so George watched over the horses until daylight.

The next day, we noticed a cloud of dust in back of us, and before long an Indian caught up with us. He was drunk and wanted us to buy him some whisky in the town ahead. We told him we wouldn't do that, and he got very angry. George settled him down with a slap in the face, and he left as he had come, in a cloud of dust.

The following day brought more excitement: Banjo again began to buck and jump, but this time we got him under control before the other animals caught the fever. Looking around, we saw the biggest rattlesnake either of us had ever seen before or since. It was five feet long and about two inches thick. We killed it and skinned it. It had a beautiful hide, very white. Unfortunately, there wasn't salt to treat the skin properly and when we unwrapped it later, we found that the skin had spoiled in the intense heat.

Neither the horses nor we were used to the dust, heat, and burning wind. That night we slept in a barn; but it was so warm we didn't sleep until early morning when it cooled off a bit. In Fresno, I gave my horse too much water, causing him to nearly lose his eyesight. Hot horses, I had forgotten, have to be watered very slowly. Because of the heat, we decided to travel by night the rest of the way to Bakersfield.

Hot though it was, our first night in Fresno was fun. We went to a shooting gallery where I won several prizes. I was a dead shot in those days. I could tell the place was crooked, because at target shooting, one little duck just would not fall over, no matter how many times I hit it. Since we couldn't do anything about it, we went out and ate a huge meal: lots of spaghetti and a bottle of wine. We were not going to need a pack horse in Bakersfield, so the next day we sold Banjo to some gypsies. Banjo was an A-1 outlaw, who used to go over backwards when we mounted him, and we were lucky he didn't do the same when the gypsy tried him out. Maybe he was tired of being pack horse for us. We hated to see him go, though, because we liked him.

After three days in Fresno, we hit the trail for Bakersfield. Ten days and a couple of thunderstorms later, we were there.

Now, we had heard about the bad conditions in the U.S.A., but Mono Basin being fairly isolated, we didn't realize things were as bad as they were. Soup lines were everywhere across the country, with thousands of people out of work. Some were called I.W.W., which stood for, "Industrial

Workers of the World," but many people called them, "I won't work," or "I want whisky." (The down-and-outers of this country will always be put down by those who have made it.)

Right away, George and I went to the ranch of his rich uncle, Mr. Gilli. He told us there was no work there for us, and that since he now had the ranch in good shape he could do the work himself. We were not invited for a meal, nor did Mr. Gilli offer us any feed for our horses, though George had spent a lot of time helping his uncle build up both this and another ranch he owned. Later, Mr. Gilli came to Lee Vining for his health and built the El Mono Hotel. It's still standing, and it looks about the same as when it was built in the 1930s. (It's now called the El Mono Motel.)

While Mr. Gilli was in Lee Vining, he did some mining back in Lundy Canyon. One of the two men who worked for him there was killed in an explosion at the mine, and that ended Mr. Gilli's mining days. Mr. Gilli's last request was that he be cremated, and his ashes emptied in Lundy Canyon, which had reminded him of the Alps. His request was carried out.

From the Gilli ranch, George and I went from ranch to ranch looking for work. A rancher finally hired George to milk his 35 cows. There were long hours and very little pay, but it was better than going hungry. There was plenty to eat on the ranch. With George working, I was on the loose, a kid broke and hungry. I used to smell the good smells coming from the bakery and wish I had just a penny or two to buy cookies — but alas! I did not.

One day, while looking for work, I came to a plum orchard by the road. The plums were so ripe that many of them had fallen on the ground. I staked my horse so he could graze, and I climbed the fence and ate many of the beautiful plums. They were so ripe and juicy. I ate and ate until I was full, and then, being hot and tired, I lay down for a nap. While I was sleeping, a motorcycle came by and scared my horse so much that he jumped around; and in doing so, he stomped on my full stomach and ribs. I quieted him down, but then I realized I was in a lot of pain. I got in the saddle again and continued on my way for abut two more hours. Suddenly, I realized that I couldn't go on. I tied up my horse and tried to lie down. My trouble, you see, was not bruised ribs, but a stomach full of plums. In short, I had a terrible case of diarrhea. Some time during that long night my condition improved and I managed to get back to town. I was recovering for days at the livery stable. I was *plum* beat!

My father back in El Reno, Oklahoma, my mother, Agnes, in

Barstow, California, and my Grandmother Mary and Uncle George at Mono Lake, California, all wrote to me. They pleaded with me to quit running around and come back home, but I was determined to go it alone, to show them I could live on my own. George Joos was still milking cows, and he lent me $2.00, all he had at the time. I think he was making a dollar a day himself.

One day I took a long ride out of Bakersfield to a place they called, "Weed Patch" (now they call it Castiac), where strong-smelling weeds grew six feet high. They had to be cut with an ax and grub hoe. Twelve or 14 men were clearing land there, and I got a job cutting weeds for $1.00 a day. I had a hard time keeping up with the grown men. From time to time, some of them were fired because the bosses, who were always watching, thought they were not working hard enough. Prunes and beans seemed to be all the Chinese cook knew how to fix — or maybe that's all they ever gave him to cook. It was the worst food ever, and the bosses were always demanding that we work harder and harder! I got so many blisters on my hands that finally, I couldn't hold the grub hoe any longer and had to quit.

I got on my horse and rode back to Bakersfield. My shoes were so worn out that my bare feet were scraping the dirt. I needed a new pair badly. Since cowboy boots were what horsemen wore in those days, I bought some. I could see that the old man at the livery stable couldn't go on feeding my horse for nothing and so I sold him for $15.00, and gave the old man half. I shipped Uncle George's saddle home to Mono Lake. Now I *really* felt lost, with no horse and those tight cowboy boots.

One morning I heard they were hiring men at the Taft oil fields. You had it made if you could get on there! They paid $5.00 a day, something to really shout about in those days! After a couple of days of unsuccessfully trying to get hired, I caught a ride on a big truck loaded with machinery. We arrived at Taft on a real hot afternoon. The truck driver paid for my meal, and I walked out to the oil field hiring office, with those cowboy boots really giving me fits. Twenty-five men, big husky fellows who looked twice my size, were ahead of me. I didn't stand a chance, but I hung around and slept behind an old shack that night. I'd taken off my boots, and in the morning I couldn't get them on again. My heels had big blisters on them; my feet were sore and swollen. I found a string and, tying the boots together, I slung them over my shoulder and started walking back to Bakersfield — barefoot. Several miles later, an old man in a little truck gave me a lift back to town, where I went to see my friend George. George gave me dinner and a couple of silver dollars.

"Georgie," said Joos, "You better go back to Mono Lake to your grandmother's ranch, or you'll die here, the way things are going for you."

"George," I told him, "if that is what it takes, I will just have to die here." I had made up my mind to make it for myself, no matter what. He saw that he couldn't change my mind, so he suggested that I go to Mr. Gilli's other ranch, near Bakersfielu. His son-in-law, Mr. Hayworth, lived there. Now, this Mr. Hayworth and his family were the same Hayworths who had been our neighbors in El Reno, Oklahoma. They had been friends of my parents back in Mono Lake. Before walking out to their ranch I went to a shoemaker in Bakersfield who fixed my boots so I could wear them. Then I bought a big bag full of hot dogs and buns and ate the whole thing sitting under a tree. I still remember how good that meal was. I walked the six or seven miles to the Hayworth ranch and got there just at suppertime.

The Hayworths were wonderful people. Besides being a preacher, Mr. Hayworth was a fine carpenter. Jobs were so scarce, he had had to stay on that little farm to keep his family from starving. They took me in and treated me like one of the family, and I tried to help out all I could. They raised watermelons and other garden produce, which Mr. Hayworth peddled at Taft. One day at daylight, we loaded his old truck with watermelons and pulled out for Taft. We covered the melons with gunny sacks soaked in water to keep them cool, and took extra water along to keep the sacks wet. When we got to Taft, we went from house to house trying to sell the melons. After all day, we still had half the load left, though the melons were large and sweet. Mr. Hayworth was very discouraged and I felt bad for him. I saw a house some distance away with kids playing outside, so I told Mr. Hayworth we should try there, as all kids like watermelons. Maybe they would coax their parents into buying some. Even there, we couldn't make a sale. On the way back to the truck, we stopped at the curb to think things over, and while standing there, Mr. Hayworth noticed something shining at his feet. Reaching down, he picked up a $10.00 gold piece!

I will never forget this incident. Mr. Hayworth was a great believer in God, and he said God was watching over us. He wanted to give me $2.00, but I couldn't take it. If it had not been for me, he insisted, he might not have found it. We celebrated by eating at a small restaurant, and we threw out all the unsold melons on the way home. After about two weeks, I decided to go on my own again. The Hayworths urged me to stay, but they didn't really need me; so I said goodby and returned to my manger at the livery stable.

I'd saved a little money, and there was a place on 19th Street where I could get liver and onions really cheap. Nearby was a hiring office with a bulletin board where jobs were posted every day. One day a notice appeared under "Farm Labor Wanted," and I applied.

I was told to stick around until more workers had applied. When there were six men (and one boy) gathered, they piled us into a wagon and we started out. After ten miles, we came to a sugar cane ranch were we were to work ten hours a day.

At long last I had a job! And the best part of it was that it was only a quarter of a mile from where my good friend visit each other quite easily.

I Get Fired — and Hired Again!

We chopped and bundled cane and loaded it in wagons. For the first two hours every morning the dew was real thick on the grass and the cane. It was foggy, too, and we got wet and cold. Later, the sun would come out and burn us, it was so hot. All of us slept in a barn filled with hay. The food was extra good, and the work was extra hard, and I was extra hungry. I was also the smallest and youngest of the crew.

Some were fired the first half-day, and more were fired in the next few days. Only the best workers were left. The farmer had a nice wife, but he himself was hot-headed and always carried a gun inside his shirt. I heard he'd had trouble years before, and was on the lookout for someone who supposedly was looking for him.

His wife noticed how tired I was each night, and she tried to make me feel better by telling me I was doing real good work. One night after supper she told me to sleep in a little back room in their home. For the first time in many months I slept in a bed. It felt so good I hated to get up in the mornings! The lady also looked after my clothes.

When the cane was all in, all the men except me were laid off. The rancher wanted me to help him make sorghum (cane syrup). We boiled the cane juice until it turned into sorghum, then poured it into five-gallon tins and shipped it out of Bakersfield by train. We worked at this 16 hours a day; and while the work was not hard, it was still a lot for the two of us to manage. The farmer would haul the first loads to Bakersfield while I kept boiling the juice. He used two mules to do the hauling, and one day he asked me if I could drive the mules. I quickly said, "Yes!" — it was a chance to get away for a day — and besides, hadn't I driven rigs back in Mono Lake on the ranch?

One bright, hot, sunny morning we loaded the sorghum tins on the wagon and I started out. Everything was fine and dandy until I neared Bakersfield. Then a car passed by and the driver gave a loud blast on his horn. This scared my mules and they took off like a shot. I knew how to saw the bits by pulling right and left; but even that didn't stop those frightened mules, and no amount of pulling the reins and footing the brake stopped them, either. They went over a high bank, upsetting the wagon. By the time I could quiet them down, half the tins had been thrown out. None of them had broken open, so the syrup was O.K.; but they were badly banged up. Unsaleable. A rider passed and I asked him to tell my boss what had happened. He said he would. I started setting the tins upright, putting the good ones in one place, and the banged-up ones in another. I was really scared, wondering what the farmer would do. Well, I didn't have long to wait. A horseman was galloping toward me. He stopped in a cloud of dust and, without even dismounting, yelled: "You're fired! Go back to the ranch and get your money!"

Knowing his temper, I considered myself lucky that he didn't beat me up or shoot me. I reached the ranch, hungry and mad, but I wouldn't go into the house. I sat down in the shade of a fig tree until the farmer's wife came running out. She threw her arms around me, told me not to feel bad, and asked why I was home. I said I was fired and didn't care. She started to cry and that made me cry. We sat together under the fig tree, crying, and pretty soon we heard a horse coming fast. It was the farmer. He jumped off his horse and ran toward me, saying over and over: "Come here! *Come here! COME HERE!*" I sat where I was.

"Damn you, come with me!" he said, leading his horse over to me. He held the stirrup out. Still scared, I jumped on behind him, and we took off on the run. When we got to where the mules were tied to the wagon with the tins all loaded, he said: "Now, hitch up those mules and get into town. Ship the good tins and bring the banged-up ones home. See if you can get there in one piece." Handing me some money, he continued: "Get yourself something to eat in town."

When I got back to the ranch, he met me with a grin and even helped me unhitch the mules and unload the banged-up tins. "Georgie," he said, "my wife and I feel real bad about the way I treated you; and I don't know how you can forgive me. If you can overlook what I did, I'd be very grateful." All his life, he said, his temper had gotten him into trouble.

I told him about my parents and relatives, who all had short fuses; and I said that I had forgotten the whole thing already — which I was glad to do.

Later, when we got the sorghum done, he took me with him to another ranch where I helped him and other men brand calves. My job was to run along the rope to where the calf was pulling, and throw the calf down. That was a hard job, but I did it! and the farmer made a big thing out of it, telling people how strong and tough I was. But then one morning there was no more work to do, and he wasn't able to pay me any longer. I'd been hired for a dollar a day, but by that time he was paying me $2.50 a day. He and his wife would keep me on, he said. I could pay for my keep by helping with chores.

After a few days I became restless, as I didn't feel I was really earning my keep. The farmer and his wife talked and pleaded with me to stay; but I had about $40.00 saved up, and I had itchy feet. I said goodby and left. I never saw those wonderful people again, but I have never forgotten them.

Back in Bakersfield, I felt rich indeed. I bought some new clothes, ate lots of liver and onions on 19th Street, and went back to sleeping in the livery stable. I treated myself to the movies and walked the town for about two weeks. Then I was broke again. No jobs to be had; not at the employment office or anywhere else. There were many hobos in town, especially down around the freight yards.

I was near the starving point again and my pal Joos had to help me out. He was still milking those 35 cows. One day, when I was down to my last dime, I blew it all on some extra long pieces of licorice. I'd eaten most of it when my stomach started to ache like mad.

I made it back to the livery stable. The old man was feeding the horses and, hearing me moan, came over to investigate. I was doubled up in real pain. Neither of us had any money for a doctor, and I was sure I was going to die. The old man said he had something he thought could help me. He brought me something in a glass and said, "Drink this." I took a sip. "Don't stop," he said, "you have to drink it all at once." I downed it. Suddenly I was on fire from my mouth to my stomach. I hollered like crazy and some men came over to see what the hell was going on. The old man explained that he had diluted Watkins horse liniment in water, because that is what he gave horses when they had the colic. I guess the fire in my body made me forget the stomach pains. The burning eventually went away, and I slept the rest of the night.

To my surprise, I was alive the next morning, and well enough to get down to the employment office.

There I saw a notice on the bulletin board under "Waiter Wanted." I had to have something to eat, so I walked into the office and asked for the job. I lied, of course, when I was asked if I had ever been a waiter.

"Yes," I said.

"Where?" came the question.

"Mojave," I replied.

"What restaurant?" they asked. I gave them a name fast. Lucky for me they didn't seem to have ever been in Mojave.

The job was at a large ranch, and I was to wait on the ranch hands.

Owned by Miller and Lux, the Buttonwillow ranch was about 20 miles from Bakersfield. It was the biggest cattle outfit in California at the time, and I was taken there by car and served a big supper. Lila, the boss lady of the mess hall, showed me to my room, a real nice one. That night I felt like a king, but I dreaded what the morning would bring. I reasoned that if all I got out of the deal was breakfast, I would have done all right.

Joe, the waiter, woke me at daylight. The place needed two waiters, and Joe's helper had been fired for being late to work once too often. Joe took me into a large kitchen where there were two Chinese cooks and one dishwasher. They showed me the very big dining room, where 40 ranch hands ate three meals a day — served by *me*. Plus, there was a little side dining room for the higher-up's: the boss lady, her husband, the foremen, and so on. Joe said he'd serve this smaller table.

It didn't take the head Chinese cook and Joe many seconds to figure out I didn't know the first thing about being a waiter. Joe had done this work for years. He could carry several platters on one arm. He helped me out all he could, but the head cook was mad and the other Chinese workers were talking about me. It was in Chinese, but you don't have to understand a language to know when you're the subject being discussed, especially when there's a good reason for it. Joe had told me that the boss lady usually didn't show up for breakfast. That was the only piece of good news for me that morning.

Somehow, I got through that breakfast and it was time for Joe and me to eat. Joe was convinced of the unsanitary habits of the cooks, and so he cooked our breakfast himself. Too soon, it was time to work the noon meal. Lila had shown up and the head cook was giving her the low-down on me. Joe said he was telling her I couldn't move the food out fast enough. "I'm afraid you're in for it, Georgie," he said.

While I was setting the table, Lila tapped me on the shoulder and said: "I want to talk to you. Follow me." We went outside and sat on a long bench. She asked me my name, among other things, and why I had lied. I told her some of my Bakersfield experiences: where I came from, who my people were. I told her I lied to get the job so I could eat a meal. That seemed to touch her the most.

Lila told me to get back to work. She asked Joe to give me a hand and teach me the ropes, which he did. He was a real nice fellow. She talked to the Chinese cook and he tamed down; but he never did like me. I made it through the rest of the day, and the following day was not quite so hard. As the days went by, I got better and better. Finally, I could hold my own, even with Joe.

The Buttonwillow ranch was a beautiful place. All its wildlife made it ideal for men. Buttonwillow paid a man $1.00 a day to go on horseback, with rifle and shells furnished by the ranch, just to try to keep the thousands of white geese off the precious grainfield. Many times, later in life, I thought I would have liked to have had a job like that. Buttonwillow's sloughs were filled with thousands and thousands of ducks, snipes, and honkers. I was crazy to hunt, but I had no gun; and anyway, I couldn't take time from work. Whenever I was free, I'd spend a few hours with the hunters, just to see all the game on the wing.

The Chinese kitchen workers smoked opium each afternoon when they took their nap. They seemed to be in a stupor for a while after they woke up. I had been working there about two months when Joe said to me one night:

"Georgie, did you ever see those Chinese go behind the cooking range when they thought no one was looking?"

I said, "No," and he said he thought they had rice wine hidden behind the stove, and that we should have a better look after they went to bed.

That night Joe found some big crocks behind the stove. In one of them, he found a gallon jug. He took it out and there was a little rice wine — *sake* — left at the bottom. We smelled it, but couldn't figure out what it was. It just smelled like something rotten. We took a small taste. In another crock we found a full jug, and then another. We took a big swig out of each jug. The stuff tasted terrible and didn't seem to have any kick at all. But we didn't give up that easy. We took some more, and some more. Still another swig, and we finally began to get some kick out of it. We talked and drank until we'd had enough. Then Joe put water in the jugs so the Chinese wouldn't miss any. (*Sake* is colorless.)

We were very happy when we finally got to our rooms, but after a short while I got sick as a dog. I fell off the bed and didn't manage to climb back in until nearly daylight, when the cold got so bad on the floor that it was a matter of getting back in the bed or freezing. I was dizzy when the alarm went off, but after dousing my head in cold water, I managed to find my way to the kitchen. Joe, on the other hand, didn't show up for work at all.

Since he was five years older than I and very strong I was surprised that the *sake* had hit him worse than it had me. I went to his bedrom, but the door was locked. I couldn't hear any sound at all, and that scared me. That morning, I did both his work and my own. Later, Lila came in and the head cook told her Joe hadn't appeared. She asked me why. I said he hadn't felt good the evening before, but I sure didn't tell her way. She went to his room, but the door was still locked; so she kept hollering until he finally answered. He still wouldn't open the door, though. Lila brought me some medicine for him. Joe just poured it down the washbowl. By noon he was able to go back to work.

That afternoon I left for Bakersfield with some of the fellows. When I returned at suppertime, Joe was all smiles. We were very busy and he couldn't tell me what he was smirking about. Every once in a while he would start laughing, and I could hardly wait until our chores were over. But still he wouldn't tell me.

"This is too good to tell you in a bedroom," he said. So we went for a walk while he told me what had happened that afternoon.

He had been awakened from his usual nap by a heck of a racket outside, near the Chinese quarters. Looking out the window, he saw three Chinese pulling at each other's long braids and kicking each other. One held a jug in one hand and kept pointing to it and then to the other two; all the time the three of them kept yelling in Chinese at the top of their voices. The one with the jug cracked it over the head of another; the jug fell and broke on a rock. Turns out that they'd all blamed each other for the watering down of the *sake*.

Lila was always talking to me. She bought me socks and shirts, too. She asked me what I thought I'd want to do some day. I told her I didn't know. She asked me to come to her house for piano lessons, but my performance didn't impress her.

In January or early February 1916, I came down with the dreaded disease they call "homesickness." I knew better than to get homesick, and always wondered afterward what the heck happened to get me that way. But that's the way it was. I told Lila and she asked me to at least wait until spring to go home.

I tried, but after a few days I began thinking of Uncle George and Grandmother Mary so much, that I had a long talk with Lila and Joe, said my goodby's, and pulled out.

I took the $35.00 I had saved up, and headed for Bakersfield. I bought a warm, heavy winter coat and heavy underwear, which took most of my money. My cowboy boots were badly worn, but I had to make do.

I trudged to the edge of town in an intense electrical storm. Luckily, I caught a ride the 60 miles into Mojave on a truck. The sky was black and threatening and the wind was blowing a gale as the driver let me off near the depot.

As I hurred past the many desperate looking hobos loitering near the doorways, I was apprehensive. Dashing inside the depot, I stayed put, looking out the window until rain obscured the view.

For several hours I waited for the train north to Bishop, contentedly eating licorice sticks and daydreaming of Mono Lake and my reunion with Grandmother Mary and Uncle George: I was going home. I was too young to know that the storm would follow me into the high Sierras, changing to an intense snowstorm with me caught in the middle of it.

Chapter 13

Home to Mono Lake

I arrived in Bishop okay. There was some snow, and it was cold. Usually, people going from Bishop to Mono Lake took the Sherwin Grade route, but a farmer had told me it was storming hard that way. He thought the road was pretty clear from Benton to Mono Lake, which was an alternate route.

I walked the four and a half miles southwest to Laws[1] and took the narrow gauge C&C,[2] better known as the, "Slim Princess,"[3] up to Benton Station — this was where the depot was located. With only a few coins in my pocket I started hoofing it, in my worn boots, toward the Sierras —due west to Benton, four miles away. The wind was blowing a gale, and just after noon a farmer gave me a lift in his wagon. He told me I had better hightail it back to Bishop, as he had heard from some Indians that Mono Lake had "heap big snow."

At Benton I helped the farmer unload his wood, and headed for the old Wells Fargo building which the owner, Mr. Davis had converted into a general store.[4] Later Mr. Davis sold the store to Mabelle and "Buster" Bramlette. They still operate it, and it is a fascinating place to visit, complete with Indian lore and antiques.

I spent my remaining coins for food, Bull Durham tobacco, and cigarette papers. I told Mr. Davis I was on my way to Mono Lake via the

---

[1] Laws was an important outfitting center for the farming and livestock industries, as well as being a mining center for Owens Valley during the early twentieth century.

[2] *C&C:* Carson and Colorado (Engine number 9) railroad.

[3] *Slim Princess:* Named by Willie Chalfant, in winter it was the only means of transportation for the area. The "catcher" usually kept the tracks clear of snow, but in extreme conditions the train was known to have left its track. It was sometimes referred to as the "peanut roaster," probably because of the billowing black smoke from its stack, due to the burning of pinon wood and coal as fuel. The track was a distance of 300 miles, terminating at Keeler on the eastern shore of Owens Lake. Engine number 9 is perserved at the Laws Railroad Museum, along with the original depot, built in 1883.

[4] As Benton Station progressed to become the permanent town, Benton became known as "Old Benton," after the mining boom had subsided and related businesses closed. New Benton is four miles east.

"Slim Princess" and crewmen. Engineer Fred Belzzar (left) later became governor of Nevada.

Benton Station, 1911.

Top and bottom: Fourth of July at Old Benton, 1912.

Dutch Pete (in top hat) with son and daughter, Emily, in wedding finery.

Mono Mills route,[5] and asked him if he had skis or snowshoes I could borrow. He said he had none to spare, but that even if he did, he wouldn't give them to me for a crazy trip like that. Eyeing my worn boots, he said I'd better get back to Bishop before I froze my feet, and he offered to let me stay the night. I was determined to go on, though, which made him very upset with me.

I was eating soda crackers when an old fellow sat down beside me. He said it was a good thing Mr. Davis was preventing me from going to Mono Lake. What did he mean by "preventing" me? I asked. He told me Mr. Davis was calling the deputy sheriff to stop me from going any farther.

When I heard this I left Benton in a hell of a hurry, running for a considerable distance in an effort to leave it far behind before anybody could stop me. I headed over the Benton range for Black Lake about ten miles away. I knew I could spend the night at Dutch Pete's. Dutch Pete's real name was Peter Guillard, and he and his sons made a fair living off their horses, sheep, and goats. He knew my folks at Mono Lake.

I arrived at Dutch Pete's at dusk and he invited me to spend the night.

[5] Mono Mills was the sawmill that provided lumber for the mining town of Bodie. There was a railroad there that carried the lumber directly to Bodie on the east side of Mono Lake. It was also where both Carlos and Joseph Filosena got their start in Mono Basin.

He told me his daughter was to be married in the spring to one of the Salque fellows. They had one large room, with a big fireplace and no stove. A huge pot of jackrabbit stew was usually cooking. The aroma was good and the taste was wonderful. There were beds along the wall. Because they had to carry their water from a spring they did not use it recklessly, if you get my point. Dutch Pete had a face full of whiskers, and he wore old, dirty clothes. We got along very well until I announced I was on my way to Mono Lake. He thought I was crazy and told me so in no uncertain terms. I told him I was convinced I could make it if I could borrow the skis that were outside, leaning against his cabin.

Dutch Pete told me that he needed those skis, but that even if he didn't he wouldn't lend them to me: "With your boots, you'll never make it anyway," he said, sounding like Mr. Davis. "Listen to me," he said, "stay here with my sons and me, at least until the weather improves. You can help us get wood for your keep, and everything will turn out all right."

Nobody can tell the young anything, as I've said before. Next morning, I started out afoot in about four inches of snow. Mono Mills was some 30 miles away. I knew the night watchman there, a man named Nort Smith.

I had not gone many miles when I was sorry I'd ever started; but I was too bullheaded to go back to Pete Guillard. When I reached Adobe Valley, I was glad to find a cabin I'd been told was there. The door was open, the window was broken and it had a dirt floor. There was nothing in it but a small stove, and above the roof the chimney was gone; but I was thankful for that.

My feet were so cold that I had to have a fire somehow. I tore some cardboard off the wall and covered the window. I shut the door and went outside to look for fuel to burn in the stove. Wood is scarce in Adobe Valley—even the sagebrush was scrawny. By dark I had found some willows along the creek and gathered enough to last me the night. I got a fire going to thaw out my feet, and ate more crackers along with some sardines. Pretty soon, the smoke started backing down the chimney. The wind had become so fierce that I thought the cabin would blow over. All through the night I sat in the middle of the room, coughing and rubbing my eyes from the thick smoke.

Toward daylight the wind stopped and snow began to fall. About this time I heard a woman's bloodcurdling scream. It lasted for several minutes. Nervously, I opened the door and hollered out into the night. When I could stand it no longer, I shot twice into the air with my .32 pistol. . . After that, I heard nothing but the wind.

The next morning I heated some snow in a can. That's all I allowed myself. I was afraid to eat the food I had, not knowing what lay ahead of me.

The wind was down and the weather clear. There were six more inches of new snow on the ground, making the snow a foot deep. Although I had intended to go back to Dutch Pete's, I changed my mind and headed out into the forest in beautiful sunshine for Mono Lake and home! About three miles away from the cabin, I came upon mountain-lion tracks. That's what had screamed so fiercely in the night, I realized.

By noon the weather picture had changed, and so had my attitude. Clouds rolled over the mountains and a cold, strong wind froze my perspiring skin from the knees down. My overalls were soaking wet from the snow, which was getting deeper all the time. I would have turned back, but I figured that by now I was a lot closer to Mono Mills than the Adobe Valley cabin. Even so, I had lost the true road in the blowing snow and was now being guided only by telephone lines. I knew that Mono Mills had a telephone, and that the lines would lead me there.

At the top of the hill, near the edge of the forest, I hit Gas Pipe Springs.[6] I was about done in at this point. I had lost sight of the telephone lines and was becoming disoriented. Recognizing that I was probably

"Slim Princess" stuck in heavy snow after jumping track.

---

[6] Gas Pipe Springs was named by Frank Pellissur, uncle of my late son-in-law, Pete Mathieu. Frank, a sheep rancher and road supervisor, installed a small gas pipe there so that water could run through it into a trough for grazing sheep to drink.

going to die out there, I ate the rest of my crackers and sardines, stomping my feet to keep my circulation going. I was terribly afraid of frostbite.

The snow became deeper, about three feet by now, and dark was closing in fast. I had trouble just putting one foot ahead of the other. Inside of my big jacket I was sweating so heavily that I pulled off my jacket and gunbelt. But as soon as the cold hit my sweaty body, I knew I would surely freeze, and so I put them back on.

On I went, falling and getting up again. It was dark and I was now completely lost in the thick forest. Nort Smith lived in a cabin somewhere on the crest of the hill, and I prayed that I'd find it.

My feet were numb. I was in another world, and had actually accepted the fact that I would never again see my Uncle George and Grandmother Mary Filosena. Each time I fell, it took me longer to get up.

Once, struggling on my knees to stand up again, I saw a light in the distance; but when I looked again, it was gone. I was dreaming. Then there was an instant of light once more; it was gone immediately. I had heard of people hallucinating just before dying, and I understood that this was what was happening to me. Suddenly, I saw the light again — only this time it stayed on and didn't seem all that far away! I put everything I had into one last effort, expecting any second to have the light go out again; but it stayed, and finally revealed the interior of Nort Smith's cabin. I stumbled and hit the door as hard as I could. Nort Smith heard me and pulled me inside. The first words I heard him say were: "I can't believe it!" and he kept repeating this over and over as he pulled off my frozen shoes and rubbed coal oil and snow on my feet to bring back the circulation.

I couldn't believe it, either! Actually Nort had been hoping I would turn up. He had received a telephone call telling him that Georgie La Braque was out in the storm somewhere, probably headed for his cabin. Soon after, the storm had torn out all the telephone lines. Smith was sure I had been forced to turn back. He was dumbfounded to find that I had actually survived to fall against his cabin door. He got the circulation going in my feet and then they *really* started to hurt. I drank lots of whisky in hot coffee and took off my soaked clothes. Nort Smith and I kept drinking the whisky and coffee, and before too long, believe it or not, I was able to walk a little and eat something. We talked until daylight and then slept all that day.

On the third day, I started out again. I still didn't have skis. Nort needed the only pair he had. But we figured that since it was warm out, I'd be able to work my way straight down to Mono Lake and follow the shoreline home. This is what I did, though it was easier said than done.

The road was still covered with three feet of snow, and it was heavy going, wading through it. It took me all day to reach Mono Lake. When I did, I built a fire on the shore and stayed all night. The tall brush made it possible for me to keep a fire going while my clothes and shoes dried out. Nort had given me food and some barley sacks to wrap my feet in, so they were in fair shape.

The next day, I followed the shoreline to Rush Creek. Several Indian horses were there, searching for food. They were nearly starved, their ribs clearly visible under the skin. I had hopes I could catch one and ride him home, but I couldn't get close enough. I followed the shoreline until I came to Chris Mattly's ranch at Lee Vining Creek. His brother Leo was there with him.

It was almost dark and I was dead tired. The Mattlys gave me coffee. Chris, apologizing, said that he and Leo had been shoveling snow off their barn, trying to prevent the roof from caving in, and would I please pitch in and help. The three of us worked into the night with lanterns. As tired as we were afterward, Chris, who was a very tough man, cooked up a meal of biscuits and salt pork and gravy for us. The bed sure felt good that night!

A day later I learned that a posse, alerted by the deputy sheriff at Benton, had started out from the Cain Ranch on Highway 395, near the south end of Mono Lake, to look for me during the storm. They found the broken telephone lines and repaired them; they had a test set with them and were able to contact Nort Smith, who told them I was safe. Some of the men really gave me hell later on for scaring everyone with my foolish stubborness. The rumor was that I had died somewhere in the snow around Mono Mills.

But no matter, I was home again! Even my pal George Joos finally got sick of milking cows in Bakersfield. He too came back to Mono Lake, where he went to work for his uncle, Chris Mattly.

Strange Bedfellows

My friend Dan Guis was what we'd call a conservationist. To give you an idea, I had seen a lost sheep on one of our treks; I was about to shoot it when Dan shouted for me not to do it. He wouldn't let me shoot diver birds for sport, either. And he wouldn't eat ducks or fish—and there were thousands to be had.

Dan had a mining claim at Conway Grade, and when he offered me 50¢ a day plus room and board to help him dig, I took him up on it. It was five or six miles away, which we walked with pack sacks on our backs. We used these for carrying tools, ore, and provisions. We cut north through the Conway Meadows and up to a cabin and a spring. Nearby, we dug a narrow tunnel about 75 feet deep. We wheeled the ore out in a wheelbarrow, and made enough money for the assessment work.

Dan's claim turned out to be a bust. The ore was very shiny, but when it was mortised, the acid ate it up: "Fool's Gold," or mica, is what it was. Dan's money ran out and we quit mining.

About this time, several Italians came to Mono Inn, near the shore, to mine in the same area we had left. A fellow named Ferris was one of them. He did not mine with the others because he could not get along with them. As he had no place to go, Dan invited him to stay with us. Ferris was strange, but most of the time we got along fine. He was hard for us to figure out. Nevertheless, Ferris and I began strip-trapping at Mono Lake. Often during the night, he would get up and wander off. Sometimes he would be gone for two days, and when asked where he'd been, he would not answer. Ferris could not speak or understand English, and when Dan and I talked and laughed about something he would think we were talking about him. Then he would sulk for days at a time. Ferris and I bought four coyote traps. He took two, and I took two. I showed him how I set my two, and then went back to the cabin. Ferris buried his traps in a big wash near the cemetery. In the morning he couldn't find where he had buried them, and he never did recover them. This made him so mad that we thought he would do something to himself or to us. This convinced me that trapping was out with Ferris.

Dan had a double barrel, ten gauge shotgun. After I'd been hunting, Ferris wanted to clean the gun. I was afraid to make him mad (I was only about 15), so I said nothing while he continued to clean it. He had a habit of leaving a rag sticking out of each barrel — to keep the dust and dirt out, he claimed. Ducks would come by all the time, as we were living right along the shore; so I would grab the gun and shoot right from our door. But I had to remember to take the rags out first, and this was a darned nuisance. I told Ferris to quit stuffing the rags if he wanted to clean the gun.

The next day I saw the gun leaning against the wall with *no* rags sticking out. I thought to myself that Ferris must surely have got the message. How wrong I was!

Ferris was outside and yelled, "Georgie, quick, get the gun. The ducks are coming!" I grabbed the gun. Sure enough, coming along the shoreline were some 500 spoonbills. I took aim and waited for the right moment, and then pulled the trigger. I expected to pull both triggers back; but as it happened, in my excitement I pulled only one. With a terrific blast the gun exploded in my hands. One of the hammers cut my ear and my left hand. My arm was cut and so was my chest. I was bleeding and somewhat stunned. I was lucky that I'd only pulled back one of the triggers. We weren't sure what the hell had gone wrong until Dan spotted one of the gun rags in the dirt near the front door. Ferris had stuffed the rags so far down in the barrel I couldn't see them. I expect you know that Ferris and I had a real row over this; in fact, I was so mad Dan had to pry us apart. Ferris left that night. A few nights later, in the middle of the night, I woke to find him looking menacingly down at me. I was so scared I couldn't have moved if I had tried. I could only stare. Then he turned and went out the door. I woke Dan and we locked the door then and there. Weeks later, we heard that Ferris had broken into a schoolmarm's home at Benton and had gotten away. Not even his old Italian friends living in Mono Basin ever heard from him again.

Right about the time Ferris left, there was a big snowstorm and I couldn't make it to Hammond's on foot or horseback; so I decided to use a crude but serviceable boat that Dan had made especially for me, mainly so I could retrieve ducks. It was square.

I rowed to Hammond's to get provisions, and had no trouble going over. On the way back I had a few problems. I had only one oar, and I had stayed at Hammond's too long. The wind was high and so were the waves. The oar came apart and the boat turned over.

I jumped out in three or four feet of water and managed to save an armful of groceries. I had to walk in the deep snow along the shoreline, and by the time I made it to the cabin my wet clothes had frozen on me.

If you're imagining that Mono Basin is a harsh, cold place to be in winter, you're right.

Chapter 14

Mono Basin Winters: Family Life

Under favorable circumstances it snows at least once every single month of the year in the little town of Mono. So uncertain is the climate in summer that a lady that goes out visiting cannot hope to be prepared for all emergencies unless she takes her fan under one arm and her snowshoes under the other.
Mark Twain — "Roughing It"

Looking back, I don't see how we did it. The ease of travel in winter in Mono County today is in direct contrast to the hazardous going in the early 1900s. It's like another world.

Mono Basin came into its own because of mining. Prospectors and fortune hunters flocked to Bodie, Lundy, Jordan, Dog Town, Aurora and other booming sites. Others, like my father, Jerome La Braque, and my Filosena grandparents came to Mono Basin to homestead and to supply food for the miners. Most Mono settlers had one thing in common. They had lived in a hostile environment before coming to America, and they were used to hardships. Traveling around the Sierras was a problem in the winter; and we simply took it for granted that we had no alternative.

Sometimes we had blistery winters with little snow; nevertheless, the highways north and south would be closed to travel from fall until late spring.

As winter swept over the peaks, we all tried to think ahead to when springtime would refresh our land. And summer in Mono is the most enchanting season imaginable.

Although Mono County is noted for its heavy snow and harsh winters, this is not always so. There have been many "open" winters. At these times, most people would rejoice. The farmers, however, would worry about water for the coming summer.

There have been Mono winters where the sky seemed to collapse in great white heaps, while trees shivered in the wind. At these times, people around Mono Basin would be faced with the test of pure survival. In the winter of 1911, the year of the terrific avalanche at Jordan, the snow was measured at eight feet at my Grandmother Mary Filosena's ranch.

We always kept a close watch on the roofs to keep them from caving in. Each home had wide, long-handled shovels which were never used for anything but snow work. We dipped the shovels in hot beeswax and resin to keep the snow from sticking. We used the same mixture for our skis. Every man, woman, and child knew how to handle a shovel.

When I was a child on the Filosena ranch, we had a hundred head of cattle and six horses. The range cattle were kept out in the open. When deep snow fell and the blizzards were on, the hay we would put down for the range cattle would blow away, and it was hard to keep them fed. Sometimes they would be without hay for several days.

During those terrible storms, with the wind pounding against my window, I used to lie in my warm feather bed (made from the feathers of Mono Lake ducks) and listen to the cattle bawling for food and shelter.

The trees would scratch their storm-beaten branches on the window pane and shivers would go up my spine, as I covered my head to shut out the terrible night.

Meanwhile, my young Paiute friends kept warm by wrapping in rabbit blankets, made mostly from black-tail jackrabbits. Once in a while I'd see a blanket made of snowshoe rabbits. These were all white, very rare, and very beautiful. The rabbit skins were rolled tightly, like a sausage, and then bound together with rawhide strips. It took several hundred rabbit skins to make a blanket, but it lasted for many years.

The land after one of these storms was a beautiful sight to behold: Mono Basin bathed in sunshine, the sky as blue and sharp as a diamond, and the earth carpeted in a glorious white.

That's when the people of Mono, each frozen breath suspended in air, would dig out. Sometimes, we'd no sooner dig out than the wind would start playing tricks, filling everything up again. On and on we'd dig, completing our chores as best we could.

After we'd shoveled off the roofs, we made paths, fed the animals, and cleared roads and trails. Then there'd be dances, card parties, and other entertainments.

Every home had a Ouija Board, and many people believed in them. Every house had a Bible and an almanac. The farmers planted by the

Uncle George Filosena with my daughter Lily on "Peanuts."

moon. No doubt about it, moon signs were a big thing for both whites and Indians. Most of us planted and fished by such signs.

In winter, we were out of school for many days at a time. I had many chores to do, so I wasn't idle on those days. Still, I put in a lot of happy times fooling around in the snow with my friends.

I will say this: back then, we schoolchildren didn't have an easy time of it. We all carried our books home and had to do homework by lamplight. Believe me, an eighth-grade education was really *something* in those days — and not many of us made it that far.

One good time was when we sat around the fire roasting sweet-smelling pinenuts, while my Uncle George would play "Home Sweet Home" and "Red Wing" on the jews harp. Most of us put pinenuts away for the winter, along with a huge supply of goods. Our cellar ordinarily held apples and winter pears from the orchard in back of the house, lots of potatoes (potatoes were Mono Basin's biggest crop), rutabagas, and carrots.

Canasta was the favorite card game, four-handed if there were enough in the family to play. We took turns playing at different homes. Sometimes there would be as many as six or eight tables of four playing. We'd get to these parties by wagons, sleighs, horseback, or skis. Sleighing was the most fun, especially on a bright moonlit night. Best of all was when we went to Christmas dances in sleighs, with the bells ringing on the horses' harnesses, and we youngsters in the back of the sleigh, lying in the hay.

In those days everyone had a good time at the dances. A huge pot of coffee was going all the time, and there were three-layer cakes and all kinds of homemade pies. The music was just one fiddle, played by Al Rule. Al later served as Justice of the Peace for many years. Sometimes Arch McKnab fiddled for the Lundy dances, with Mabel Montrose, a Lundy girl, accompanying him at the piano.

Most of the men looked like hippies of the sixties. They usually wore beards and Levi's which only cost 85¢ or $1.00 per pair. These were never washed, but were worn until they wore out or fell apart. Our underwear was woolen, red, and doublebreasted. Heavy, warm outer clothing was a necessity, along with good footwear. We had half-inch heavy felts (liners) inside our high rubber boots. The Paiutes were not so lucky. Their shoes consisted of burlap bags wound in strips around their feet. Yet, somehow, they got by.

One of the bearded dandies was John Mattly, Chris's cousin. John seldom missed a dance. He was Mono's first postmaster, in 1889, when the post office was located at Mono Inn. He sported a long, grey beard of which he was very proud. He generally kept it rolled up and pinned under his chin with safety pins. But whenever he went to a dance, he unfurled it. It hung to his knees, and as he swung his partner, the beard would float out into space. It was truly a spectacular sight!

Somehow, in spite of John's sprightly appearance, he could not find a suitable bride; so like many men, he advertised for a wife. A Mrs. Benedict, a widow, answered his advertisement; and after some correspondence and an exchange of photographs, Mrs. Benedict and her son Ed, arrived in the Basin. She and John were married, and they settled on his ranch near the Jordan Power Plant, where John started a small dairy, beard and all.

I was only 14 when I would ride Scookum up to the Lundy dances. I would stop by Carter's boarding house at Lundy Dam to pick up my 12-year-old friend, Jimmy Carter.

Jimmy and I would double up on Scookum and ride to Lundy, where we'd put our horses in the livery stable.

Mt. Snowdon, overlooking old town of Lundy.

Many of the dances were square dances and waltzes, and sometimes, the Shotze. Jimmy and I did not dance; we enjoyed watching, and kicking up our heels, mostly around the tables piled with sandwiches and cakes. His older sister Edna, always danced with Harry Anderson from Poverty Flat, whom she later married. Liquor was never served at the dances, even those held in the mining towns. If liquor was used, it was drunk outside the hall and in very small amounts.

At dances in those days, when the musicians' time was up at two o'clock, collections were usually taken up so they would continue to play; and play they did, often until the sun came up. On one occasion, the dance Jimmy and I had gone to did not end until about nine the next morning.

Jimmy and I headed for the livery stable to get Scookum and go home. But Scookum had other ideas. He was feeling ornery. I got on first and hoisted Jimmy, who was dressed in his best, behind me. Scookum gave a big lurch that tossed Jimmy down *spang* into a pile of fresh manure. He got to his feet and tried to wipe himself off, but the damage was done. Mournfully, he declared, "I'll bet Mom will sure be *mad!!*

I helped him back up, and we were soon at the boarding house. When I left him off, I didn't stop to find out, I just kept on going.

I ran Scookum the rest of the way home, as it was high time for chores. We had chickens, pigs, and a mean cow named Fanny. She once charged Uncle George, tossing him over the fence. The only thing that saved him from serious injury was his sheepskin coat. My crippled Uncle George did a lot, but the heavy work was left to me. Grandmother Mary worked in the house mostly, making butter, and of course, cooking and canning. We used to warm the newly hatched chicks behind the kitchen stove in a little box. It was fun to watch them peeking shyly out, chirping contentedly.

After the chores I was treated to a glass of fresh warm milk accompanied by a chunk of yellow layer cake with chocolate frosting. On Sundays, we usually had chicken and an Italian dish called "Polenta." This was a stiff corn meal mush, covered with a meaty tomato sauce, topped with grated cheese.

Mary's Italian Polenta

Bring 4 cups water to boil. Add salt to taste. Reduce heat. Add two beaten eggs to three fourths cup of milk. Add to mixture along with one cube of butter. When blended, add one cup meal — Polenta or yellow corn meal. Stir frequently until thickened. (A double boiler may be used.) Pour into greased casserole, top with a generous amount of grated Jack or Cheddar cheese and bake at 350° for about an hour and a half. Top with meaty tomato sauce.

Meaty Tomato Sauce

Saute one chopped onion in olive oil, bacon grease or lard. Add two cans tomato sauce (or 1 can sauce and 1 can whole tomatoes). Add two cups water, pinch of salt, pepper and oregano. Boil an hour and a half, then add meat, which may be prepared while sauce cooks.

Flour and brown pieces of meat in hot skillet. Use chicken, cottontail rabbit, duck, sage hen or quail. Drain fat and add one cup water. Cover and simmer slowly until tender. Cool and remove meat from bones. Add to prepared sauce, cooking 20-30 minutes more. Spoon onto hot polenta, topping with cheese if desired.

Left-over Polenta may be sliced and re-heated in the oven.

Sometimes my grandmother had a hard time getting around because of her rheumatism. Illnesses like that called for home remedies; childbirth demanded a midwife. One of the midwives was Mrs. Jake Mattly. As a matter of fact, she delivered yours truly. Teeth were pulled with pliers: you did it yourself or called for a relative. Mustard plasters or sliced onions were common poultices for chest colds. Liniment alleviated rheumatism and sore muscles, and of course, there was "Lydia Pinkham's" for the women."

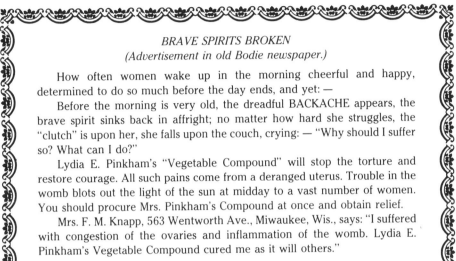

BRAVE SPIRITS BROKEN
(Advertisement in old Bodie newspaper.)

How often women wake up in the morning cheerful and happy, determined to do so much before the day ends, and yet: —

Before the morning is very old, the dreadful BACKACHE appears, the brave spirit sinks back in affright; no matter how hard she struggles, the "clutch" is upon her, she falls upon the couch, crying: — "Why should I suffer so? What can I do?"

Lydia E. Pinkham's "Vegetable Compound" will stop the torture and restore courage. All such pains come from a deranged uterus. Trouble in the womb blots out the light of the sun at midday to a vast number of women. You should procure Mrs. Pinkham's Compound at once and obtain relief.

Mrs. F. M. Knapp, 563 Wentworth Ave., Miwaukee, Wis., says: "I suffered with congestion of the ovaries and inflammation of the womb. Lydia E. Pinkham's Vegetable Compound cured me as it will others."

Contrary to what you may hear, whisky really was used for snakebites and over-exposure. It helped get the circulation going again. I personally knew two or three people who were saved from snakebites by whisky. My father, J.B., once bought a bottle of medicine from a traveling medicine man which cured him, and he had been very ill.

Indian tea, *ephedra* ("e-phed-ra"), was used profusely, especially for kidney infections and bladder ailments. It was even claimed to cure veneral disease. The needles of the tea plant were steeped in boiling water. One advantage of Indian tea was that it could also be dried for winter use. It was used as a general tonic, and it is still being used by many of us today.

The greatest remedy of all was Mono Lake water and, later, Mono Lake salts. Cuts, sores, dandruff, rheumatism, or arthritis could be helped by taking several dips in Mono waters. Ladies found it wonderful for washing their hair.

Only one telephone line connected the Mono Lake post office to Bridgeport. This was a single line on a pole, and bottles were used for insulators to hold the wire. Mr. Bryant, Dan Bryant's grandfather, and an old-timer of Bridgeport, owned the line. It was out of commission most of the winter. When the roads were passable, Dr. Kelly could be called to come over from Bridgeport. He had a great fondness for Schnapps; so usually folks had to give him a great pot of coffee before he could tend to the patient.

When the doctor's ministrations failed, the ill were loaded on a toboggan pulled by several men wearing skis or snowshoes, and either taken to Bodie, 25 miles east, or to Bishop, 60 miles south. It usually took two full days just to get to Hot Creek, the halfway point to Bishop, where the caravan usually spent the night. They would continue on the Sherwin Grade where the patients were transported by car the last 12 miles to the Bishop hospital.

Many Indian men were hired on most of these winter trips to help pull the toboggan. They were very tough and uncomplaining although they suffered from their burlap footwear.

Snowshoes came into use in Mono around 1914. They were preceded by "bear-claws." These were made out of willow, perfectly round and laced with rawhide cross pieces and foot straps in the middle. They were good in rugged country. Later, the "webs" came into use. This was a nice, easy shoe to travel on. Webs were about four feet long, made of rawhide, with a factory-made hardwood frame. They had foot straps near the middle. It was a very useful snowshoe. I myself used them on my trap lines at Tioga and Gem Lake.

One of the best skiers at Mono Lake was a Canadian, Louis De Chambeau. He had bought a ranch from Carlos' former partner, Decius. This parcel was adjacent to my Grandmother Mary's ranch. Louis had a hard time coaxing a living out of the land, so he added to his income by making skis. He was such a fine craftsman that he always had a backlog of orders. The skis were made of soft white pine, four inches wide and six to seven feet long. Louis sold the skis for $5.00 per pair, plus $1.00 for a long pole which was about 5½ feet long and 1¼ inches thick.

This pole was essential for descending steep hills. Holding it firmly with his hands, the skier would let it trail between his legs, more or less sitting on it and bearing down heavily to slow down, turn, or stop.

The halfway stop to Bodie was the "Goat Ranch," named for Canadians who used to raise goats there. An Italian, Joe Scanavino, had come from Dayton, Nevada to buy it. Joe and his wife operated a stage

The Scanavino family, with Joe, schoolteacher (middle), and Mrs. Scanavino.

Ruins of Petrali ranch.

stop at the ranch, offering hot meals and lodging to travelers. Equipment could be repaired there and horses stabled, fed, and watered.

One traveler told of a humorous incident he had witnessed at the Scanavino ranch. Joe was not to be seen and the traveler asked where he was. Mrs. Scanavino angrily declared that she had banished him to the woodshed because of his suggestion to send to Italy for another wife, so as to increase the number of children who could help out on the ranch, which was several hundred acres. They already had five or six children of their own, and she took a dim view of the proposal. (Joe was always known as a great kidder.) His friends, however, insist that he couldn't have stayed in the woodshed very long (or too often) as the Scanavinos ended up having 12 or 13 children.

Joe, always a great one for progress, built the first school in Mono, especially for his children, about 150 feet away from their home. The Scanavinos furnished board and room for the teacher.

Bread for the family was made once a week. A fifty-pound sack of flour was used; the bread was baked outside in a sheepherder type of oven.

To the east of the Scanavino ranch there was a large spring where three Italian families had small ranches. They were Petrali, Roux, and Carnonica.

They made their living primarily by raising dairy cows. the milk was shipped on the Bodie railroad which ran from Mono Mills past them on its vay to Bodie.

Like us, these folks eagerly looked forward to mail deliveries, which were very uncertain during the winter months. Needless to say, the rugged mail carriers were much admired and respected. When mail service was interrupted, one felt cut off from the rest of civilization.

 Chapter 15

Carrying the Mail in Winter

It wouldn't be fair to tell you what Mono Basin was like back then without mentioning some of the mail carriers and the adverse conditions they worked under.

Regardless of the famous post office creed that nothing keeps a carrier from his appointed rounds, etc., the deep snows and heavy fogs of Mono Basin did indeed keep mail carriers from making speedy deliveries. Lord knows they tried hard enough.

Many times a carrier became lost in a blizzard or dense Mono fog. Miraculously, only a few perished. These intrepid carriers of the mail were not deterred by the icy winds, or wet, sleety snow which perpetually stung their faces.

The stage drivers bid for jobs, with the lowest bids getting the federal contract. Those hired were required to have ther own horses and equipment, as well as the basic know-how to run a stage line winter or summer.

When winter weather prohibited the stage from operating, rugged men took over the deliveries. They were paid by the pounds of mail

to Wellington and Mound House

CONWAY STAGE STN.

35

(STAGE ROUTE via SWEETWATER CANYON)

East Walker River

Devil's Gate

ELBOW STAGE STN.

WILLIAMS STAGE STN.

9 MILE RANCH

SUMMIT STN.

15

to Hawthorne via Lucky Boy

GREEN'S RANCH

FLETCHER STN.

SHARPS STAGE STN.

"Mail 🐛 Stage Routes

LIME KILN ROAD

Bridgeport Dam

DELLMONTE

AURORA

Bridgeport

SUNSHINE STN.

POTATO PEAK

BODIE MTN.

BODiE

HANK BLANCHARD'S TOLL HOUSE

MURPHY STN.

MURPHY SPRING

LOWER MORMAN CABIN

MORMAN RANCH STN.

COTTONWOOD CANYON

CABIN FOR SHELTER

HWY. 167

DOG TOWN

BRIDGEPORT CANYON

COYOTE SPRING

GOAT RANCH

Legend

● RANCH

▲ Stage Stop

★ Town

3/4 INCH = 4 MILES

MONO DIGGIN'S

RANCHERIA GULCH SPRING

HECTOR STN.

HWY 395

OLD BODIE R.R.

N

LUNDY

CONWAY RANCH

WILSON

CURRIE'S RANCH

FISHER

Mono Lake

WARM SPRING

(TIOGA LODGE)

HAMMOND'S (TOLL)

NEGIT IS.

PAOHA ISLAND

carried. Using skis or snowshoes, these men carried from 60 to 80 pounds of mail on their back.

The Bridgeport-Mono Lake route, by way of Moorman ranch (a large stage stop), was said to be the worst route in winter. The route continued on to Deep Wells and Murphy Springs, where the horses were watered, and then on to Hector Station. It ended at Fisher's (Danburg Beach). Currie ranch later replaced Fisher's as a stage stop. At Currie's there was a large barn, where a Portuguese fellow named Tony took care of the horses. It was a treat to stop there, as Tony could usually be heard playing his mandolin and singing.

One of the drivers I knew on this route was "Big John." He was six feet tall and weighed 250 pounds. John was one of the few carriers rugged enough to handle this route in winter. Exceptionally well liked, he was calm and pleasant, often going out of his way to do many favors for the people along his route.

John Dondero, Sr., who was exceptionally strong and good with horses, worked winters at Hector Station. One winter's night while on the way home to the Filosena ranch during a blizzard, I arrived at Hector Station. I took John's friendly advice and stayed the night, enjoying pot-luck dinner with him. I remember how warm and snug the small cabin was, even though the storm was raging outside.

The worst route of all was from Mountain House, Nevada (seven miles north of Topaz on Highway 395) to Bridgeport, via Wellington and Sweetwater.

"Jeffries" was the carrier who had this route. No need to tell you, he was one tough man. Mountain House was a main stop, serving meals and even lodging people when necessary.

Leaving Wellington (going south), one of the main stage stops was Conway Stage Stop, which was run by Pat Conway. This stop had stables, food, and lodging.

The Mono Lake-Lundy route originated at Fisher's, and later, at the Currie ranch. It was impassable a good deal of the time in winter. When open, it was run by Casey, a short, barrel-chested Irishman. He was known as a tough man in a fight, of which he had many. Casey enjoyed his whisky, and when he was "in his cups," he could often be heard singing Irish ballads.

Cecil Burkham had another hard go. The route from Hawthorne, Nevada to Aurora and on to Bodie. There were three stops: Fletcher, Sharp's Station, and Del Monte. Del Monte was a large stop outside of Bodie, with stables, several inns, and a blacksmith shop for repairs. They

Della Dondero Hern of Mariposa, California.

say it was Cecil who, seeing how the horses floundered and sank in the deep snow, came up with the idea of putting snowshoes on them. Cecil told the blacksmith of Bodie, Oscar Snider, how to construct them. The shoes were a square foot around and were fastened to the hooves with a special clamp.

At first trial, the snowshoes did not work too well; but Cecil kept experimenting and finally got one team going that did very well on them. The horses were trained in the summer, out in the fields. If a horse threw a shoe while traveling, it was very hard to get it back on. But the horses would wait patiently for the driver to shovel it out and refasten it. I never knew a horse to break a leg with the shoes, though many did get hurt.

The most well-remembered carrier and mail driver of the Mono Lake area was Charles Fulton. He was extremely rugged, and quite a character.

"Charlie," as we all call him, began this type of work around 1916. He was a surveyor; and he worked as both mail carrier and surveyor for Mono County for over 20 years.

When Charlie had a surveying job, he'd hire someone else to carry

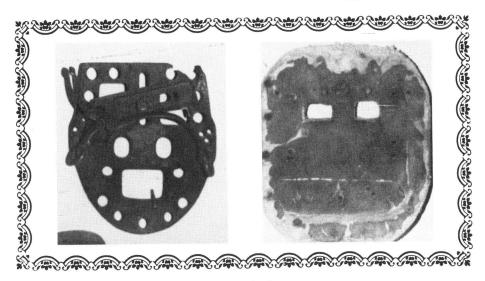

Snowshoes for horses.

the mail. He was a huge monster of a man with a lean frame and large, square hands. A long, olive drab coat (which looked like an Army issue) flapped around his feet, and the outfit was completed by a wool stocking cap with a stripe, pulled low on his forehead.

Even in the frostiest weather Charlie seldom wore gloves. He handled the mail sacks with his bare hands. His only condescension to the weather was a lantern that he placed directly under the seat of his sleigh. Meanwhile, any friend hitching a ride sat on the opposite seat with teeth chattering.

Charlie held many contracts for different routes through the years. One of his routes, taken over from "Big John," was from Bodie, via Del Monte and Aurora. He usually drove two horses and a sleigh, but if the load was extra heavy, he used four horses. The mileage was ten miles going over and ten back. In bad weather Charlie had to leave at 7:00 a.m., not returning until midnight. It was a sixteen-hour day, rough all the way.

Charlie's "home base" was where the town of Lee Vining now stands, in the vicinity of Murphy's Motel. He had a small, neat cabin, and a barn with a large, fenced area for his many horses. He owned two acres there, and more meadowland east of Highway 395.

Every winter Charlie, who was the County surveyor, surveyed the snow behind Twin Lakes Craggs, in the back country near Bridgeport. The elevation at the survey site was 11,000 feet. It was 22 miles, uphill, to

Mail carrier Charles Fulton with team and passenger, Bodie.

the site, by way of Buckeye Canyon; and it was all done on skis. The complete trip took a week or more.

Robert (Bob) Bell, a native of Bodie (now living in Luning, Nevada), was hired by Charlie as a "swamper" on these jaunts. He carried the supplies and assisted in the survey. Bob had worked in the Bodie mines as a lad, with his dad, an assayer.

Bob describes Charlie as a "tough old rooster," and recalls that Charlie's skis did not work at all well, as they had no points. Most of the time they were so far under the snow that one couldn't tell if they were still on his feet; but Charlie took no notice of this and moved right along. A square cabin afforded them shelter at the top of the Craggs. Because of the formidable snow depth, the door was on top, near the chimney. The sampling tool consisted of four sections of alumnium, which they coupled to make a pole 20 feet long. Samples were taken in three different spots. The surveyor would leave a marker so he could use the same location next year.

At times the depth of the samples was 180 inches — 15 feet deep! Bob was paid $20.00 for a week's work, the going rate at that time.

While surveying, the men carried only a piece of bread tied to their belt for lunch. When food ran low Charlie cooked up a concoction of rice and raisins, laced with a generous splash of whisky. Bob, unimpressed by this culinary delight, protested vigorously whenever Charlie stayed longer then usual in the back country.

In later years, Charlie used an old Chevrolet panel truck for mail deliveries; and usually its brakes did not work. Using a zig-zag route, he would streak into Bodie like a rocket, pass the Post Office by 20 feet (until the brakes took hold) and then back up.

Bob and a friend were once driving a short way out of Bodie when they saw Charlie coming toward them in a cloud of dust. Knowing Charlie's truck, the friend threw his car in reverse and started backing up as fast as he could. Even at that, Charlie stopped just a couple of inches from them. As I said, he was a real character — with lots of good character, though.

One day, while Charlie was driving his sleigh and horses, he counted four horses instead of two; in fact, he soon began seeing two of everything and had to retire. In five or six years, our old friend Charlie was almost totally blind. He stayed on in Lee Vining for many years, I'm happy to say.

One of the "super-men" of yesterday was a mail carrier long before my time. John A. Thomson, the famous "Snowshoe Thomson." performed almost impossible feats over snowbound trails day and night, carrying 80 or 90 pounds of mail some 90 miles through untracked Sierra Nevada wilderness, with the snow 30 or 50 feet deep. His route was from Placerville to Carson City, and on to the new settlement of Genoa. His skis were ten feet long and four inches wide, and were said to weigh 25 pounds. He made his first trip in January 1856. When the snow softened, he was forced to wait (sometimes a week) until it hardened again. "Dope" (ski wax) was practically unheard of in those days. Each skier had his own "secret" formula for waxing skis, which usually consisted of a combination of pitch, tallow, and other ingredients, applied to the bottom. People said of Thomson, that if he was not the swiftest man on skis, he was the most expert. His record of 1600 feet downhill on crunching, icy snow was 21 seconds. He was the only mail carrier I ever heard of who used "moccasins" for his skis. These were made of bed ticking and slipped over the back half of the skis to prevent them from sliding backward as he went up steep hills.

After 20 years of service at $200.00 a month, Thomson began to feel Congress owed him a debt of $6000.00 or so for underpayment. (There was no retirement or Social Security in those days.) So he filed a claim. Congress sent him a nice letter of thanks but no money.[1]

---

[1] "Snowshoe" Thomson is buried at Genoa, Nevada; his skis are on display at Sutter's Fort in Sacramento, California.

Chapter 16

Trouble at the Filosena Ranch

In 1915, Grandmother Mary and Uncle George became unfortunate participants in a problem with some Mexicans at their ranch. I had just turned 16 a few months earlier, and was working on the Tioga Pass road as a teamster, pulling a "stone boat."[1] This is the way the trouble came about.

During the year, two local developers (working independently) sold parcels of land on the northeast and southeast shores of Mono Lake to would-be settlers from outer areas. The parcels proved to be a part of a sandy, waterless desert. The developers planned to bring water to them by means of two ditches.

One ditch was started from Rush Creek, on the south, which followed the base of the Mono Craters.[2] It was sandy and so time consuming it had to be abandoned. The rock work, along with the sandy ditch bed are visible as one travels east on Route 120.

A second ditch on the northeast side, originating from Lundy Creek (formerly Mill Creek) was planned to deliver water at the northeast development of Warford Springs.

Around 17 to 20 Mexicans were brought in to dig this ditch. Their camp was a mile or so from the Paiute Indian camp, on a small hill just north of the Filosena ranch.

The Mexicans were simple laborers from a revolution-torn country where "law" seemed to be whatever the strong wished it to be. They worked hard and played hard.

---

[1] *Stone Boat:* a sled made of steel, three-eighths of an inch thick, three feet wide and flat, attached by chains to a team of horses. It was used to dump excess slag over the side of a roadbed or to haul rocks for retaining walls. It was also useful in the removal of rockslides.

[2] *Mono Lake Craters:* a chain of 21 extinct volcanoes, mostly at the south end of Mono Lake. Negit and Paoha Islands, as well as Black Point at the north end, are all part of this chain.

The Mono Craters.

Remains of dry ditch at base of Mono Craters.

I often competed with one of the crew, a young fellow named Teddy, at the Sunday afternoon shooting matches held at Hammond's. As I remember, we were well matched. Most of the Mexicans were peaceful, but not all. Some enjoyed raising hell and not worrying about the consequences. They would celebrate on Sundays by getting drunk. And sometimes, they would ride through the tall brush near the Paiute village, swoop down on a young girl walking along the trail, ride off with her a suitable distance, then rape her.

The Indians were angry about the way their women were being abused, and they held a pow-wow to decide what action to take. Before they could act, however, the pot boiled over at the Filosena ranch. It was Sunday, July 25. A girl named Sal, who often did chores at the ranch, passed by late in the afternoon carrying her weekly provisions from Hammond's store. She stopped to ask grandmother Mary for some *hogadie*, the Paiute way of asking for food.

I don't doubt that Sal made a pretty picture as she ate her *hogadie* out on the front porch. She had a pink glow to her dark skin, set off by shiny black braids. She wore many layers of colored skirts. Sal picked up her tote bag and started toward her camp. She had just crossed a deep, wide irrigation ditch, when two Mexicans grabbed her and pulled her back to the ditch bank. Even though she struggled and kicked, she was no match for them.

After her ordeal, Sal was fighting mad. She fought and kept screaming for help. The rapists' mood became ugly. They shoved her into the ditch and held her head under with their heavy boots.

Luckily, Pete Roberts, the hired hand, heard her. He rushed into the house, grabbed his twelve-gauge shotgun, and ran toward the ditch, where the rapists were still trying to drown Sal.

As Pete closed in, the rapists pulled knives. Pete was small but tough. He dazed the closest one with a blow from the gun stock. He lashed out at the second man, and he, too, went down.

By now, the first one was coming at Pete again with a knife. Pete wrenched the knife away, but dropped his gun. Both men grabbed for it, but Pete got to it first. He brought it down with such force on the man's head that the gun barrel bent, making it useless. Blood poured from the man's mouth and Pete wondered if he was dead.

My crippled Uncle George arrived and helped Pete pull Sal out of the ditch. She was limp, and not breathing, and they were sure she had drowned. Pete gave her a crude sort of resuscitation, lifting her up and down until water began to dribble down the corners of her mouth. She began to stir, and in a short time, they were able to help Sal limp back to her village. Miraculously, Pete had only a few cuts and scratches.

The rapists came to, staggering to their ponies, and headed home. Pete told Mary and George to expect some kind of retaliation from the Mexicans that night.

Taking a blanket and another shotgun to the orchard behind the house, Pete spent the night in ambush. Just before daylight, figuring the Mexicans were not coming after all, he returned to the house. Fifteen minutes later there was a knock at the door. It was the Mexicans. Their speech was slurred with liquor as they shouted, "Gringo, you come out!" Then George shouted, "Go away or there will be trouble." The angry Mexicans retorted, "You sons-of-bitches are going to have plenty of trouble if *he* doesn't come out! We give him one last chance."

There was a flare in the darkness. The barn and haystack were on fire. The Mexicans were kicking at the door and calling for Pete to come or they would burn down the house. They doused the house with gasoline and set a match to it.

Inside, Mary and George were terrified. They called upstairs to Pete, who was trying to get a bead on the Mexicans from the window: "We'll have to go out; we can't stay here and roast like pigs." Slowly, they edged out the door as the Mexicans stood by, expecting Pete to follow.

Unhindered, Mary and George managed to put out the fire with water from the ditch.

It was now almost daylight, and the Mexicans were becoming uneasy. They knew that Mary's neighbors would notice the smoke and come over to investigate. Shouting rapidly in Spanish, they mounted and rode south. The fire in the barn was out, but much of the hay was destroyed.

George rode bareback a third of a mile north to a neighboring ranch. Albert Silvester, a deputy lived there. After listening to George, Albert rode quickly to the Thomson ranch. Deputy Allen, who had one of the only telephones in the Basin, called Jim Dolan, the Mono County Sheriff. He was 25 miles away in Bridgeport. Allen advised him that there was a "Mexican uprising," and to get down to the trouble spot quickly, as the Mexicans were heavily armed.

Meanwhile, when Jim Duffy opened his general store at Mono Inn that morning he found it ransacked. Whisky, shells, food, and a pair of hob-nailed boots were missing.

Word spread fast, and many ranchers and Indians gathered at Duffy's and Hammond's. Before the trouble was over, three men would be dead.

Young Sheriff Jim Dolan.

Sheriff Dolan Is "Dry Gulched"

It was 5:30 a.m. when Sheriff Jim Dolan received the S.O.S. from his deputies. Dolan woke "Pud" Waltz, owner of the local livery stable. Pud acted as Dolan's chauffeur.

Armed with an old .45 automatic pistol, Dolan and Pud drove off. They stopped at the Filosena ranch just long enough to find out the facts, noting that the two Mexicans had been seen riding south. Pete Roberts warned the Sheriff: "Take no chances; they'd just as soon shoot a sheriff as not!"

Other men offered to ride along, but Dolan felt that there would be less chance of a shoot-out if he went alone. He was dead wrong.

According to Waltz, they stopped at Hammond's for a few minutes.[3]

---

[3] Waltz's account is based on the version reported in the *Carson City News*, July 28, 1915.

Native-American artist Raymond Andrews captures the violent episode at the Filosena ranch which led to Sheriff Jim Dolan's death.

L. to r.: "Pud" Waltz, Sheriff Dolan, and friend in front of Mono County Courthouse.

No one was up but the Chinese cook. While Pud was talking to him, Dolan noticed two men with sombreros heading south a few hundred yards ahead on the road. He took his automatic from his holster, cocked it, and put it on safety; then he tucked it back under his belt. Pud and Dolan drove slowly after the Mexicans, down the road bordered by wild roses.

As the car approached, Pud stopped at the spot where the road branched off toward the Nay and Mattly ranches. The Mexicans turned into the brush, pausing on a small rise. Dolan told Pud to act as if something was the matter with the car, so Pud busied himself under the hood.

The Mexicans continued to watch as Dolan stepped down from the car. He folded his arms with his hand on his pistol, and took a step toward them. "Boys," he called, "I'm the Sheriff. I want to talk to you."

The one who spoke English said, "What is the matter with your car?"

Dolan ignored the question and repeated, "I want to talk to you. I want you to give yourselves up."

One of the Mexicans had a rifle; the other had a revolver. Before Dolan had finished speaking, both Mexicans fired. The sheriff staggered and turned as two more shots were fired. Dolan was hit, but he did not fall. He tried to fire his pistol, but it jammed, leaving him helpless. Also, one of the bullets had exited through his gun hand. Dolan dropped his gun and staggered into the willows as the outlaws escaped through the sagebrush.

"Are you all right, Chief?" called Pud Waltz.

Dolan answered, "I took two bullets. Get help, but don't drive. You might get shot, too."

Pud ran down the road to the Chris Mattly ranch at Lee Vining Creek.

When Pud and Chris reached Sheriff Dolan, they found him lying on the front seat in a large pool of blood.

They carried him directly to Hammond's and summoned physicians. Dr. Ware of Bridgeport and Jim's young wife, Cordelia, were first on the scene.

Dr. Crebs of Carson City, Dr. St. Clair of Reno, and Dr. O'Neal of Bishop arrived some hours later with nurses and surgical appliances, and immediately held a consultation. Two bullets had passed through the Sheriff's body. A third had exited through the right hand, having entered at a point above the elbow. The large intestine was almost completely severed. The doctors prepared for emergency surgery.

After the operation, Dolan became delirious; but during one lucid spell he gave out this statement: "The one in the gray coat shot first," he

Dolan's operation took place at Hammond's. Friends wait around for outcome. The cars are a steam-operated Franklin and a Packard.

said, not realizing how critical his condition was. He kept blaming the jammed automatic for his failure to get off a shot.

As the night progressed, Dolan's conditioned worsened. He died at two o'clock in the afternoon.

Cordelia said later that something had wakened her suddenly at ten minutes past seven, and she had sat upright in bed. She had been uneasy, but had gone back to sleep. When Jim Dolan's watch was removed from his pocket, it was found to have stopped at ten minutes past seven, the exact time of the shooting.

Francis Burke was deputized, and with a posse of eight men was soon on the trail with Ranger Fred Clark and Warden Baurder.

Clark took the lead, as he was best acquainted with the terrain. At Horse Meadows the posse lost the trail. They scattered out into parties of two and three, hoping to pick it up again.

John Dondero, Jim Duffy, and a man named Strong were covering the area near Brand's Lodge.[4] As they came out of the willows in the meadow, they spotted the fugitives higher on the slope. They were using a large pine tree for cover and had their weapons drawn. They had Dondero's group covered.

Dondero, noticing some cows grazing nearby, and realizing that there was no chance for the posse to use their rifles, shouted, "What in the hell is the matter with you fellows? Why do you want to shoot us? We lost some cows and are looking for them. We're not here to bother anybody!"

Dondero's little speech probably saved their lives. The Mexicans called back, "All right, we believe you. There are men after us, and we're going to fight."

The three posse members turned and slowly rode down the trail, not daring to look back and expecting a bullet in the back any minute. Dondero's horse unseated him and ran away, and he had to continue on foot.

Later in the afternoon, the three rejoined the rest of the posse at Hammond's. They assured the others that they would be in for a fight to the finish.

It was dark now, and the posse disbanded until daylight. Meanwhile, during the night, many other volunteers arrived.

An old Indian named Jimson had a ranch at Lee Vining Creek. Jimson was known as the best tracker in Mono Basin, and also as the best shot. The posse decided they needed him. They took him to the spot where

---

[4] Brand's Lodge is known today as "Berger's."

Dondero and his group had encountered the Mexicans, and he soon picked up the trail. There were now about 200 men in the posse, broken up into many different segments.

Jimson tracked the fugitives through the Jake Mattly ranch and on down to Rush Creek. They appeared to be headed toward Mono Craters.

A discarded gray coat was found. Hob-nails in the boots worn by one of the Mexicans left distinctive markings in the sand and made tracking easier. Boots like these had been stolen from Duffy's store.

The Mexicans had cut across what is now Highway 120, heading southeast toward the base of the third crater. It seemed a strange direction for them to take, but Jimson insisted that this was the case.

The Mexicans were very tough. They'd been up all night and they were still going strong. Jimson began finding signs that they were resting from time to time. Whisky and a lack of water were weakening them.

Jimson expected the Mexicans to take the road toward June Lake, and that they would be found in the sagebrush soon. But instead, the trail led Jimson and the posse straight toward the craters.

Following the trail at a gallop, the posse soon entered the timber at the base of the largest crater. Jimson said, "No one can get very far up that crater. I will stay here; you fellows go ahead. They are very close." Just a little farther on, the battle was about to begin.

Only three hundred yards now separated the posse from Sheriff Dolan's killers. It was a grim race.

The posse closed in: Francis Burke, Fred Clark, Will Farrington, Jim Duffy, M.C. Stromer, John Dondero, Royce Bristow, and one other, name unknown. All were mounted.

The killers had been lying behind a log, napping and drinking. One had his shoes off. When they caught sight of the posse they drew their guns in a fight for their lives. Instead of using the log as a shield, they fought standing straight up, bandit style. Their first shot grazed Bristow's chin and knocked him off his horse.

Immediately, the posse scattered and took cover, with the exception of Stromer, who dropped to his knees and began shooting.

One of the killers fired a shot at young Will Farrington, who was lying on the ground within ten yards of the bandit's barricade. The bullet pierced a can of Prince Albert tobacco in his pocket.

Will got off a shot with a .30-.30 mushroom bullet and killed one of the Mexicans. The other was keeping up a hot fire, shooting Duffy's horse out from under him. A bullet tore a hole in one posse member's britches. Then Stromer put the remaining Mexican out of action with a good shot, and the other posse members finished him off.

The bodies were taken to the schoolhouse at Crater,[5] where an inquest was held that night by the Justice of the Peace, Pearl Mattly.

The verdict was that the Mexicans were killed by a sheriff's posse while resisting arrest.

It was learned that the Mexicans were Juan Francisco, age 50, and Theodore (Teddy) Solido, age 22, my former friend and shooting partner.

A miner named Alex Ross made the coffins, and the two men were buried the next morning on a little rise between the Jake Mattly and Farrington ranches. For many years the graves were marked by a wooden fence, but time and weather have eliminated all traces of the spot.

L. C. Brand, a Los Angeles millionaire, who owned the lodge where the Mexicans were first spotted, flew up in his plane, the *Mono Eagle*. He came to Hammond's and gave $20.00 to each member of the possee.

Sheriff James P. Dolan was in his mid-thirties when he was killed. He was buried on July 29, 1915, in the Bridgeport cemetery. His widow, Cordelia, was a schoolteacher. Faced with the prospect of raising and supporting their two-year-old daughter, Alice, and of paying the doctors who had treated Jim, Cordelia petitioned the court for the $4000.00 death benefit which she assumed would be forthcoming, as Jim had certainly lost his life in the line of duty.

Due to a legal technicality, she was denied any compensation.

After Jim Dolan's death, concerned citizens held a public meeting to decide on a new sheriff. Sentiment ran high for the slain young lawman, and many people were determined to have his brother Bert, take his place. In due time, Bert Dolan was sworn in, serving Mono County for the next 20 years with the same qualities of fearlessness and devotion as had his brother.

Covering a span of some 25 years (1910 through 1934), the Dolan brothers became a legend, adding their names to the list of the finest early lawmen of the West.

Where was I during all this? I had just finished breakfast at Tioga camp when Mike Drew, a Paiute, rode in from Mono Lake.

"Have you heard the news?" he asked.

"What news?"

"Mexicans pretty nearly burned your folks' ranch down last night," he answered. "And Sheriff Dolan's been hurt.

I hurriedly told Mr. Stone, my boss, that there was bad trouble at our

---

[5] Crater is now called Farrington Meadow.

Brand's "Mono Eagle," first aeroplane in Mono County.

Jim Dolan (right) in his office with unknown friend.

Sheriff Bert Dolan.

ranch and that I had to get down there. I ran all the way down to the meadow past Headquarters Camp at the foot of Tioga Pass, where I had my horse pastured. With only a half hitch and no saddle, I rode toward the ranch, stopping at Hammond's for about five minutes. I learned that Sheriff Dolan was on the verge of death.

When I reached the ranch, 40 or 50 people were milling around in the yard. I was relieved to see that my family had not been harmed.

I formed a posse of one, strapping my rifle on my back. I had a hunch that the fugitives would head toward the craters. I rode through the Nay ranch, on to Lee Vining Creek, to Rush Creek and on to the Samman ranch. I saw no sign of them, but I did hear a volley of shots several miles south.

It was late and I was tired out; so was my horse. I started back and met an old Paiute on the trail. I said I was looking for the Mexicans and asked if he has seen them. He said, "No, but I hear shot — maybe somebody die!" He gestured toward the craters.

I rode as far as Hammond's, where I saw men mounting their horses. They called out, "No more outlaws to look for. They're already dead. The posse shot 'em full of holes. And Jim Dolan just died," they added sadly.

I rode with them as far as the Filosena ranch, where all the trouble had started. I was dusty and beat. My folks had learned of Sheriff Dolan's death. It grieved us all. The *Bridgeport Chronicle* (November 20) carried the following epitaph to the well-loved lawman:

Tioga Pass, early 1920s, vicinity of Blue Slide.

"Headquarters" camp of Southern Sierra Power Co. at base of Tioga Pass.

**IN MEMORY OF
JAMES P. DOLAN**

——— —

When God ordained that we should live, He also willed that we should die. These laws are immutable. The babe in the cradle smiling through transient tears; the youth with life's bright expectancies animating him to action; the vigorous man full panoplied for the fiery fray and eager for the battle; and the aged with their allotted time past, are every moment subject to the call.

James P. Dolan, our friend, and when we say our friend, we know we voice an undivided sentiment of all who knew him, has answered this last early call.

'Twas a shock that made our hearts stand still when the news came of his untimely ending. Just as life seemed the most propitious. His spring days gone and an auspicious July day nearing. The battles with struggling fortune won, he bade it all good by.

We ate silently by kerosene lantern. I remember we had fried potatoes (my favorite) and boiled meat. We talked into the night, and then I mounted up for my ride back to Tioga camp.

When I got there, I left my horse in the meadow to graze and hiked slowly up the steep pass in the moonlight.

Chapter 17

Of Mines and Men

In 1916, an outbreak of rabies was reported in Mono County. One morning, my Uncle George went out to feed the pigs, carrying two buckets. He didn't notice anything unusual until he came face to face with a coyote sitting betwen the cow corral and the pig pens. It didn't move; it just sat there looking at him. Knowing well that this was not normal behavior, he approached cautiously. When he got closer, he could see the coyote was foaming at the mouth. He rushed inside, grabbed his gun, and shot the animal.

The town of Aurora in Nevada was booming for the second time. George Wingfield, the big mining man from Nevada, was responsible.

Several hundred people were in Aurora at the time. It was a nice little mountain settlement, surrounded by pines and meadows. A large red-light district flourished toward the west end, alongside of the original town. The new part was over the hill from the Magnum Mine's forty-stamp mill and cyanide plant. The mining company had built small houses for its employees.

My Uncle George helped me get a job in the mine working with my two good friends, George Joos and Evert Mattly. Uncle George loaned me his horse Peanuts, and early one morning I started out bareback toward Aurora by way of the lime kiln back of Mono Lake. At Aurora, I would board with my Aunt Mary Donnelly and her husband, Frank, who worked in the mine. They lived in one of the company houses on the pine-covered hillside along with their two small daughters, Doris and Florence, and their son, Clifford.

When I got about ten miles from Aurora, I turned Peanuts loose as my uncle had instructed me. He would find his own way back home. I watched the big clouds of dust he made as he ran. I continued on foot up the trail. As I looked toward the top, I was startled to see a coyote loping down the trail in the bright noonday sun; especially with me walking straight towards him.

Right away, I remembered the rabies scare and quickly looked for cover; or at least for some rocks to throw. The sagebrush was very short; there were no rocks to be found. My heart pounded as I jumped off the trail and lay real still. And it was none to soon. The coyote passed me very close. I saw its open mouth, the tongue hanging out, dripping foam.

I was safe but scared. I moved fast, running to Aurora in record time.

The town was quite orderly when I was there; but it had apparently been as wild as Bodie, where the inhabitants were said to "kill a man every morning, before breakfast."

I'd heard that a young girl, accompanying her father to Bodie, where he was going to work at the Standard Mine, had heard of the mining town's rip-roaring past. She is said to have prayed, "Goodby God, we're going to Bodie." Others say she was misquoted. She had really said, "Good! By God! We're going to Bodie!"

At the Magnum Mine we were mining gold, using the zinc process to extract it from the ore. My job was learning to operate the "ball mills." The operation worked this way: a conveyor belt moved the ore to the stamp mill. The stamps were above my work place. They were heavy metal crushers that pounded up and down in piston-like fashion, breaking the large rocks into smaller pieces. These, in turn, passed into the ball mill, which crushed them into a fine concentrate.

Bodie miners with lunch pails, early 1900s.

Lime kiln, north of Mono Lake.

The ball mill consisted of long steel tumblers, with iron balls that rolled inside as the tumbler rotated. From this the ore was passed over a mercury table, where copper plates picked up the larger pieces of gold. The fine gold and concentrate that the table did not pick up were put into a cyanide solution and packed into large tubes.

The cyanide solution which had picked up the gold was mixed with a zinc concentrate and put into 40-pound buckets, where it was shipped to a smelter so that the fine gold could be extracted. The buckets were worth about $250.00 apiece, and were sometimes stolen by "highgraders," or dishonest workmen.

It was a very nice mill and a good place to work. I was soon able to take over as a tube operator.

I became friends with the stamp mill operator on my shift, a fellow by the name of Spriggs, who had a wife and six children. Once, when I nearly lost my life by almost falling into a cyanide tank, Spriggs took me out to his house for a visit and gave me a good talking-to for being careless. He was a good friend.

Something happened to me about this time. I confided it to Spriggs, but until now no one else has ever been told.

One night while I was working, as was my custom around 2:00 a.m., I wandered down by the cyanide tanks, just looking around. From where the big tanks were, you could look down on the press floor where buckets of zinc and gold mixture were kept. They were stored in the open with electric "hot" wires around them. Anyone who tried to get the buckets could expect to be electrocuted. I noticed a movement below on the press floor. Two men were removing buckets from within the electrified circle. One man was passing them to another. A third man was at the conveyor belt receiving them. I watched as they took five or six buckets. Apparently, an accomplice on the inside had temporarily cut off the electricity.

I must have moved. One of the men noticed me and pointed in my direction. The men disappeared quickly into the conveyor room. They couldn't have been any more scared that I was, though. I knew they would take drastic action to keep me from reporting what I had seen. Maybe a beating, or worse!!

The next day, I opened up to my friend Spriggs. He was very worried. I was so afraid, I would not go to work by myself. I was especially nervous about working the night shift.

I don't know what might have happened had Spriggs not suffered a horrible accident. I'm glad I was sick in bed that night, so that I wasn't one of those who witnessed it.

At the entrance to the mill was a cable that lowered the ore car down the rails from the top of the mill to the bottom. We all had to step over it everytime we went to work. This night, Spriggs tripped over the cable, falling down on the ball mill. On the tumblers were long bolts that stuck out. These held the heavy metal plates inside the mill and kept the tubes from wearing out. When Spriggs fell, those bolts decapitated him. He was thrown onto another ball mill and his body was torn to pieces. When I went back to work the next night, I imagined I could see him still, waving to me from his platform.

There was no social security, welfare, or insurance at the mills in those days, so my friends and I took up a collection for Spriggs' wife and children. We gathered several hundred dollars. Afterward, I asked for my time, because I knew I could never work there again. The boss asked me to stay on another week and break in another man for my job. I did, but it was the longest week I ever spent. I picked up my wages and left right away at a jog-trot, heading for my home in Mono Lake, 32 miles away. I bought a bag of food from an Aurora café; and when I reached Bodie, I ran right on past into Bodie Canyon without stopping.

It was a warm fall day, and my money belt was getting heavy. I had been paid off in gold and silver, as was the custom. My gold pieces felt heavy, and I began to wonder how many of them were in my belt. When I got to the bottom of Bodie Canyon, I stopped by the stream to drink and rest a bit, and count my gold pieces.

First, I looked up and down the road to make sure no one was in sight. Then I took off my money belt and shook out the gold pieces. They sure were beautiful! Just as I started counting, I heard laughter on the hillside above me. A voice called down; "Did you rob a bank?"

I looked up, and not 75 feet away were two men on horses, looking at my gold. I was so scared, I couldn't even talk, much less run. Down they came to the stream and got off their horses. They knelt down to drink, then walked over to take a closer look at my shiny gold. They could tell I was scared, because one of them said, "Don't be scared, boy, we won't rob you."

They sat down and rolled Bull Durham cigarettes, tossing me the makings, and I smoked also. When I was able to get back my voice, I told them I had got paid off in Aurora and that I was on my way back home to Mono Lake. After a while I put my money belt back on, and said goodby.

They told me they were cowboys working for Mr. Burkum, the cattle rancher. I never did learn exactly how much money I had until I got to my grandmother's ranch. Even then I ate first, as I was very hungry. Then

I poured all my coins on the table . . . five-, ten-, and twenty-dollar gold pieces. It amounted to something like $250.00, which was a fortune in those days, when farm wages were $2.00 a day.

I was glad to be home again; but the country was soon in a turmoil about going to war with the Germans, and everybody was talking about the draft. My buddies George and Evert left their jobs in Aurora to come home to Mono Lake. They knew they could be called up at any time. The three of us decided we'd trap and have a good time before we were called to the service, so we set up a camp at a big old house at the lower end of Rush Creek, near the shore of Mono Lake.

For several months we had a merry time hunting and trapping. There were lots of ducks, geese, and rabbits for food, and Evert was a good cook.

George and Evert did get called up, but I was too young. Eventually, I got a notice to be ready to report in 48 hours. Jack Preston, Glenn Mattly and I left together to enlist at Los Angeles; but when we arrived we were chagrined to learn that the war had just been declared over.

George and Evert arrived home in good shape. George returned to the Mattly ranch, where he helped his Uncles Chris and Leo, mining salt at Mono Lake. This was quite different from the usual mining. It meant boiling the Mono Lake water over a hot sagebrush fire. It was a very hard and tedious way to make money, but it was a lot safer than mining gold.

Some of our Mono friends didn't make it home from the war and there was great sadness in the valley for a long time.

Chapter 18

Patrolman on the Flat

Early in the winter of 1918, I took the job of patrolman for the Southern Sierra Power Company. I was a lineman out on the flat about three miles southeast of the Cain ranch near the base of the Mono Craters, and I had a cabin there. The power lines from Silver Lake, Mill Creek, and Bishop came together at this point. The lines at Poole Plant, up in Tioga Canyon, and at Mammoth Lakes, to the south, were not yet established.

The main switches for testing the different lines were at my station. When I located which line was in trouble, I would head out to find the breaks and repair them. In winter I did my trouble-shooting on skis. During the summer I rode horseback. Later on, the linemen used "weasels" (a type of tractor), and still later, snowmobiles. I worked the job in the "good old days," when we considered ourselves lucky just to keep the telephone lines open. My job was to patrol both power and telephone lines.

From my cabin I patroled halfway to Hot Creek, where there was another cabin and another patrolman. I needed a team every ten days or so to haul drinking water to my cabin. I had to be on the lookout for trouble during storms; but on good days I could visit the Cain ranch, or my grandmother, or even Hammond's store. I always had to tell the control station at Bishop Creek, which was run by a Mr. Kaatz, where I was going. Lee Montague ran the Cain ranch power station for the Southern Sierra Power Company. He also did line work for them; and I usually could get him to take over for me while I was gone.

My wages were only $120.00 a month, but there were fringe benefits — like Bingo, for instance.

The man I replaced had a dog named Bingo, which he left with me. Bingo was about a year old then, and right from the start he turned out to be one of the best dogs I ever had.

Not that Bingo didn't cause me a lot of trouble. But he was never more trouble than he was worth. I really loved that dog.

151

One winter day I rode down to Mono Lake to shoot some ducks for supper. Immediately, Bingo was out in the lake, bringing my ducks to shore. A duck dog was really necessary in those days; you might even say a matter of life and death, if you recall how my friend Evert Mattly died. If Evert had had a dog like Bingo that day on Mono Lake, he wouldn't have had to strip off his clothes and swim into the freezing water for his ducks. And maybe he'd be alive to laugh with me today.

During my first winter as patrolman, there were severe windstorms that brought deep snows. It was the worst winter people had seen for many years. The wind ripped out power and telephone lines. I couldn't reach Mr. Kaatz at Bishop control, and no one could contact me. I rode over to the Cain ranch, where Lee said he would work on the telephone lines going to Silver Lake. I headed out south for an emergency cabin at Dead Man. There were three switches there, and when I had them repaired, I hoped to contact the control station at Bishop.

The storm was over. When I got out of the Mono Lake fog belt, the day was nice and sunny. On the way to Dead Man, I found power poles down, and stayed in the cabin there the first night.

In those days, only single poles were used, and they were none too strong at that. This storm laid them flat from Hot Creek to Bishop and out on the sand flats toward Benton as well. No phone connection could be made anywhere.

The next day, while fixing the phone and power poles at Sand Flats, I met the Hot Creek patrolman. Together we worked on the lines, he going back in his direction and I in mine. All that day I mended broken lines. The second night at the Dead Man cabin I made contact with the Hot Creek patrolman, but no contact could be made with Kaatz at Bishop. On the third day, we finally contacted him. By now lines were up all the way through. Tough Lee Montague must have been really busy at his end.

Now came the big problem of getting the power poles back up. A crew started out from Bishop; but at the top of Sherwin Grade, the snow was so deep they had to pull their supplies by toboggan, using a long rope and many men. Lee and I organized a repair party at the Cain ranch. We got a crew of about 20, most of them strong Indians. At first we tried a huge sled and four snowshoed horses to pull it. Snowshoes for horses consisted of square pieces of flat iron clamped onto the hooves. While our horses didn't break any legs, they kept losing their snowshoes. We finally gave up on the horses. Men would have to take their place pulling the toboggan.

We loaded our supplies on three toboggans. A long rope was attached to each toboggan. Ten men with shorter ropes around their waists were fastened to the main rope on each toboggan. One of the crew was a tough Paiute by the name of Joe McBride, and I remember that another was Bridgeport Tom. Also, there were Caseuse, Silas, myself, and many others whose names I do not remember. The cook was an Italian named John Bilie. The snow at Dead Man measured seven feet; and it was about three and a half feet at Hot Creek and the Cain ranch.

The first day out was long and hard. We made it halfway to Dead Man, starting from the Cain ranch. Poles had to be erected and wires needed to be spliced. At Dead Man, where we arrived the second day, we camped three days, fixing transmission lines and fallen poles. Halfway to Hot Creek we camped a few more days, eventually meeting up with the Bishop crew. All of us spent the night at Hot Creek, our job completed for the time being. The rest of the poles could wait until spring; but we'd have to get at them early, because many were broken off very short, making them dangerous to anyone who might come too close.

Back at the Cain ranch with our empty toboggans, we paid off the help. Lee and I had a long rest.

I made my regular rounds, carrying with me a telephone test set, extra wire, pull tackle, pole climbers[1] and tools, and something to eat. My patrol became more routine.

Before very long, however, the telephone lines went out again, so I took my test set and headed out the south route. Even before getting to Dead Man, I had found the break and fixed it. I continued to the cabin, where I ate my lunch; then I headed for home. When I arrived, I discovered that I had carelessly left my telephone test set back at the Dead Man cabin.

I immediately called Lee at the Cain ranch to tell him I was without a test set. His own was broken, he said, and the replacement he'd ordered had not yet arrived. That left both of us without a test set. I was very upset with myself. At eleven o'clock that night, I called Mr. Kaatz at Bishop control and told him I was heading back for Dead Man. He told me I was crazy to set out in the middle of the night like that. A storm was on its way and he thought I should at least wait until morning. I was so mad with myself, though, that I couldn't be dissuaded. I was determined to retrieve the test set.

I took Bingo and started out on my skis. The moon was out, the skiing was good, and I made it to the Dead Man cabin just before daylight. I built a fire in the stove and made myself some coffee. I picked up my test set

---

[1] *Pole climbers:* Sharp metal points that strapped onto the leg and dug into the wooden telephone poles.

and started for home, arriving there just before noon — just as the big storm finally came crashing down. I write about this because from that moment, I learned to think about what I was doing. I had been too careless before. Mr. Kaatz thought I was one hell of a young man, because the four trips I had made that day totaled about 30 miles, more or less.

I was about 19 years old and exceptionally strong for my 5'6" height. To be honest, the ladies really took a shine to me. My black hair was thick and wavy, and my attitude — well, you might call it "devil-may-care." I fancied the ladies no less than I hoped they fancied me.

Springtime was easier. I patroled on horseback, and sometimes I would ride over to the Cain ranch to visit Lee. I also found a lot of reasons to visit the Jake Mattly ranch: they were boarding a young schoolmarm from Los Angeles by the name of Hilda Boron. I used to pick up her at Jake's and we'd ride double back to my cabin. I had only fourth-grade schooling, and I knew I needed to educate myself. I'd brought a typewriter and was learning to spell. Everyday I learned several new

George Dewey LaBraque, age 22 years.

words to increase my vocabulary. Hilda thought this was wonderful, and she encouraged me.

Whenever I would visit Lee, I would leave my dog Bingo back at my cabin. Lee's dogs were big and Bingo couldn't handle them. On my return, Bingo would jump as high as my saddle to greet me. When I went to pick up Hilda, I usually left Bingo at home. Carrying two was okay for my horse, but Bingo made it a "crowd." One day, though, he followed me all the way. On the way back, Hilda and I had other thoughts to think, and we didn't notice that Bingo was following too close. Accidentally, my horse kicked Bingo and broke his hip. We happened to look back and saw him lying in the road.

Hilda rode on to the cabin, while I carried Bingo in my arms. Seeing that I was ready to cry, Hilda put her arms around me; and that *really* made me bawl. I shaved off the hair on the injured side, made splints, and put Bingo in his bed. Three weeks later, Bingo was able to walk, and I took off the splints. He was still very lame, but I couldn't bear to think of losing him.

One day Mr. Kaatz called me from Bishop control to say some men had reported seeing flashes on top of the big transmission switch at Hot Creek. This switch had given us trouble before. The patrolman at Hot Creek had had to climb up and reset one of the blades on the switch using a stick, because after the switch was opened, it was difficult to reset. The patrolman was in the hospital, Mr. Kaatz said, so I would have to go and fix the transmission switch myself.

Next morning I was off early on horseback, headed for Hot Creek, about 22 miles south. I was traveling on about a foot of old, hard-packed snow. I was moping as I always did when I had to leave Bingo alone with his bad hip, even though I'd left him plenty of water and food to last until I got back. Halfway between Dead Man and Hot Creek, I noticed my horse looking back, so I turned to see what was bothering him. There was Bingo!! He was limping after me as fast as he could go in the snow! Furthermore, he had broken his hip all over again!!

Gently, I tied him to the back of the saddle and went on. It was dark by the time we got there and we stayed overnight in the cabin. In the morning I reached in my pack for my climbers. They were gone!! My climbers had evidently fallen through that hole. No big deal, though; I shimmied up the guy wires, and with a large stick, tapped the blade into position again. I knew where the trouble was, as I had seen the switch arcing in the night.

I tied Bingo behind the saddle and rode toward my cabin on the flat, arriving just before dark.

Mr. and Mrs. Jake Mattly.

The Jake Mattly ranch, three miles south of Lee Vining.

The first thing I did was to reset Bingo's leg. This time I kept him quiet for about six weeks before I took off the splints. I kept close watch on him, and several times a day, lifted him and turned him on his other side. After many days, he was able to take a few steps, and about a month later he was walking around outside the cabin. Three months later, Bingo could run and play again, though he had a real bad limp the rest of his life.

Hilda and I became engaged. I rented Phil Lorenzo's best team of horses from the Mattly ranch to take my fiancée to meet Grandmother Mary and Uncle George. At the ranch, my grandmother prepared a chicken dinner for us, while Uncle George played the jews harp. After an enjoyable evening we started home. About a mile north of the Mattly ranch, as Hilda and I were mooning about, I carelessly dropped one of the reins. The horses tore off into the sagebrush, turning the wagon over. Both of us were thrown to the ground, but neither of us was seriously hurt.

It was a great relief to find the wagon was okay. Phil never knew of the upset, and I did not hasten to advise him of it.

After several months I began having second thoughts about getting married. Times were hard and I was doubtful that I could support a family. Hilda was eight or nine years older than I. We mulled it over and concluded that marriage was not a good idea, after all, and Hilda returned to Los Angeles.

We corresponded for a while. I missed her terribly. I decided a change of scene would do me good; so I sold my typewriter and told Mr. Kaatz to get a replacement.

Lee Montague took Bingo; and as a matter of fact, when I returned to visit years later, I was amazed to see that the little dog recognized my voice even before he saw me! Bingo jumped wildly on me in greeting. We were both delighted to be reunited.

Lee and Bingo had obviously become very attached to each other, so I left them together. Lee told me how, when I'd left, Bingo wouldn't eat for days. He'd wander over to the cabin on the flat looking for me.

I left for Oklahoma shortly afterward, to see J.B. I had not laid eyes on my father for ten years.

Chapter 19

Hard Times

When I arrived in El Reno, I learned that J.B. had taken a job with the railroad. We had a lot of catching up to do. I told him how I had been spending my time at Mono Lake; he dispensed fatherly advice. Don't gamble (do as I say, not as I do, of course); don't drink; don't fight; and above all, no wild women.

I listened respectfully, but not much of it sank in.

It was about this time that the flu epidemic started in the United States, and I was not spared. One day, while I was sitting in the barber chair getting a haircut, I became real sick. I spent the next few days in bed with flu; and it took me another week to recover.

There weren't any jobs available in El Reno; besides I missed the ranch and my Mono Lake pals. I decided to return. Before I got on the train J.B. and I had our portrait taken together.

My ticket was for Carson City, Nevada. I would stay there to visit my Filosena grandparents: Charlie and his second wife, Mary. They had three young sons. One of the boys, Lester, was only a year younger than I. We became good buddies and roamed around together for half a century.

It was early winter when I reached Carson City. The flu epidemic was not so bad there, though back East people were dying every day.

I began gambling heavily. Maybe it was in my blood. I would work hard; then when payday came, I'd promptly lose all my money. Gambling was the only thing I thought about.

I had some money when I returned from Oklahoma, but it didn't last long. I immediately lost it in a five-card stud poker game. Charlie's wife was an easy-going woman, but my grandfather was just the opposite. He gave me a severe tongue-lashing for going broke. I took the hint and left on foot for Mono Lake, with four inches of new snow on the ground.

I was anxious to see my grandmother and Uncle George, as I had been gone for many months; but nobody I knew would lend me any money to leave town. As I hung around the depot, I heard they were

My father and I, El Reno, Oklahoma, 1918.

hiring section workers at Lake View, a few miles south of Carson City. This was on the Virginia and Truckee (V&T) narrow gauge railroad.

I set out on foot late in the afternoon. It was snowing and very cold. It was early evening when I arrived at the home of the section boss, Mr. Norton. He was surprised to see me looking for a job so late in the day.

He looked me over, and right away informed me that the job required big, tough men. To help me out, though; he said that if I could board and room at the Burger home[1] close by, he'd try me out. The other section workers all lived in Carson City, as there were no lodgings at Lake View. Mr. Norton advised me to think it over first, saying again: "It takes real men for section work. It's a nine-hour day, and very hard labor."

The job paid $2.50 a day. There was no need to think about it; I was determined to take it. At the Burger house, Mrs. Burger said she was sorry, but she had no room for me. She explained that although their

---

[1] The Burger home is located at the top of the hill, about six or seven miles north of Carson City, on Highway 395.

house was large, it was brimming over with their eight children. Besides, she had too much work to do to take on a boarder. I said I needed the job badly. Could I sleep in the woodshed out back?

The Burgers left the room for a few minutes. They must have sympathized with my plight, because they came back and told me I could have the woodshed, warning me that it was unheated. They figured I wouldn't last a day at the job, anyway. Everybody knew how hard the work was, even for grown men.

I not only lasted out the first day; three months later I was still on that section crew, working from early morning until nearly dark. I was still sleeping in the icy woodshed — and still gambling!

We worked mostly in Washoe Valley, between Lake View and the old town of Franklin. Washoe Valley is one of the worst places to be during a Nevada winter, plagued as it is with cold winds and snow.

Mr. and Mrs. Burger treated me like one of their children. Mrs. Burger filled my lunch bucket every day: mostly with jelly sandwiches because they were so poor, but plenty of them. Joe Burger tried to persuade me to stop gambling, but I was deaf to such talk.

Recently renovated "Joe Burger" home at Lakeview, Nevada.

I had been there about two months when the flu epidemic finally hit Nevada. The number of deaths was increasing every day. Many businesses were temporarily closed, because so many workers were ill.

One of the little Burger girls was the first in the family to get it; and one by one, they all went down, including Mrs. Burger. Mr. Norton was the only well man on the section, besides me. Doctors didn't know how to treat all the sick; and the doctors who weren't sick themselves were so busy it was hard to find one.

At the Burger home, I took care of Mrs. Burger and the eight children. Mr. Norton had said he hoped I'd stay and help them out. I told him the last thing I would think of was leaving the sick family. We all figured I had developed an immunity to the flu because of the light case I'd had in El Reno.

When Mr. Burger came down with it, I became nursemaid to ten very sick people. I was on duty 24 hours a day, bringing wood to keep the house warm, brewing hot tea and lemonade. I have no idea how many glasses of hot lemonade I made for them. Clarence, the oldest boy, had the worst case. One night I had to tie him to his bed, he was so out of his head with fever. I feared he would be dead before morning; but by dawn the crisis had passed, and he recovered. So did the rest of the family, which I considered a miracle.

Gradually, Mrs. Burger was well enough to help me, and I got some much-needed rest. Corpses were piled high in Carson City.

Luckily, my own relatives all lived through the horror. I lost three friends, though. Gradually, the epidemic died down and people got back to work again.

I was back on the section crew — and back to sleeping in the woodshed.

"Go-devil" Days in Virginia City

One night after supper, Joe Burger was reading the Nevada newspaper. "They're starting up one of the old mines in Virginia City," he said to his wife. "They must mean business; they're hiring miners and fixing up the mine shaft."

I took all this in, but said nothing right then. The next night, after thinking about it in the woodshed with the wind howling around me as usual, I made up my mind to try for a job in Virginia City. When I told Joe, he laughed like hell at the idea. Since jobs were so scarce, only the biggest, strongest miners were considered for hiring:

"When they look at your size, and see how young you are, that will be the end of you."

Joe, however, had also told me that Mr. Norton said I could hold my own with the best when it came to section-hand work. Another crew member had told me that the mine job would be easy compared to what I was doing on the section crew. The pay at the Virginia City mine was $5.00 a day — twice what I was getting.

It sounded good to me.

Although the winds were howling full blast that night, I was so dead tired I couldn't keep from sleeping. The sound of these winds so impressed themselves on my brain, that for years afterward, even to this day, I get nervous when the wind blows.

Mr. Norton gave me the day off and told me not to be disappointed if I wasn't hired, as he didn't think I had a chance. Nevertheless, I was in high spirits as I caught the train for Virginia City.

When I arrived at the Comstock Mine office at 10:00 a.m., there must have been at least 200 men there. The man who did the hiring stood above us on a platform, so he could look us over for size, age, and physical strength. He would point at a man or call out several in the crowd.

I was not one of them, of course. Discouraged, I moved away and sat on a large rock to plan what to do next.

Finally, all the men who had not been hired left, except *me!* The boss was inside with the men he had picked out for work. They came out and left, followed by the big boss, about 15 minutes later. I hadn't planned to speak to the big boss, but something got into me. I stood up and blocked his path.

He brushed me aside, but I kept following him. Suddenly, he turned to me and snarled: "What the hell do you want, anyway, kid?"

I said, "I'm no kid, and I need a job."

He laughed and said, "I suppose you're one of the best miners in the West, and that's why I should hire you. Right?"

"Mister," I said, "I've worked in tunnels; I've baled hay; and I've held my own on the railroad section at Lake View."

He could not believe his ears, and paused to ask me how long I had worked at Lake View. He said, "I can't believe you ever worked there. That's the hardest job there is."

I told him to call Mr. Norton, my boss, and ask him. As it happened, he knew Mr. Norton well. He was very surprised.

"How the hell is that Irishman, anyway?" he asked.

I told him Mr. Norton was fine and dandy.

Jovially, he slapped me on the back and said, "Kid, I'll put you on. I don't know why, but I just want to see how you work out. Come to work on the 3:00 p.m. shift this afternoon."

My work clothes were at Lake View, I explained; but if I could go to work like I was, I'd be there on time. He laughed again: "Go get your clothes, kid, and report tomorrow at 3:00 p.m."

I was so happy I could have run all the way back to Lake View.

Joe saw me get off the train, and walked to meet me. "Well," he said, "what happened?"

I told him I got the job, and I told him the details.

"I can't believe it," he said. "Come in the house and tell the Mrs. about it."

Mrs. Burger was surprised and glad for me. I ran down to Mr. Norton's cabin and told him, too. He hated to see me go, but he was glad for me, too.

"Wait a minute," he said. Going to a table in the room, he wrote something and sealed it in an envelope. "Give this to the boss who hired you," he said, and grinned.

When I got to the mine next day, I gave the envelope to the boss. When he read what was inside, he laughed and laughed. I sure would like to have known what was in that letter!

Three o'clock finally came. I got to the shaft with many other men. I confess I looked like a shrimp compared to them, and they coolly gave me the once-over. I climbed into the cage and down we went to the 2800-foot level. How that cage did travel! It felt like my legs were going to go through my belly when it braked to a stop.

Down at the work level I was told what to do and what not to do. Candles and lamps burned everywhere. The temperature at 1500 feet was over 100 degrees. The workers wore as few clothes as possible, and their bodies glistened with perspiration.

Our safety equipment consisted of a head covering — a narrow rimmed hat, to keep the dirt out of our eyes — and heavy shoes to protect our feet from the sharp quartz. Steam and hot water poured from cracks in the rock. There were blowers that forced cool air down to us in pipes two feet in diameter. In spite of this, we were able to work only half an hour at a time; then we'd rest for half an hour. While resting we drank several quarts of water and chewed ice supplied for this purpose. Falls were the common cause of death, for some men fainted who couldn't tolerate the sudden changes of temperature as they surfaced. The shaft went on down to 3300 feet; but they'd had to give up working at that level, because of the excessive heat. The ore at that level burned your hands if picked up without gloves.

In the old days there was so much high-grading going on that wages had been only a small part of the pay; but when I worked there, there was no high-grade left, and we worked only for wages. The heat didn't bother me too much after that icy woodshed. It felt like heaven!

I was paired up with a big Pole, mucking. Before a blast, the drillers would set a steel plate down, and after the blast we'd shovel off the plate. There was good air circulation and the heat was only bad if you shoveled too fast. I could shovel with the big man easily. We took turns rolling out the huge ore car when we got it full. The rail track where we had to push the car curved sharply. I only weighed 130 pounds, and I usually got stuck on that curve and had to ask for help. This made my partner mad. He didn't much care for me, anyway. I think it was because I was out-working him right along, except for pushing that car. He grumbled to his pals, and I'm sure he also talked to the foreman about me.

Once in a while the big boss would come down into the mine and stop and chat with me. One day, he asked me how I was getting along, pushing the car out. I knew right away that the Pole had said something. I said, "Okay," and nothing more was said; however, sometime later the boss came down again and told me he had an easier job for me, running the "go-devil."[2]

The foreman told me how to run it, as well as where in the tunnel I had to get the loaded cars to take them to the main shaft. When the cars had been hoisted to the top, the ore was taken to the mill. This was a real easy job; but it did not have the half-hour break.

I took my room and board at a Chinese place, where I also did my laundry. I remember the food was greasy. By this time Virginia City had already seen its hey-day, and there couldn't have been more than a couple of thousand people living there. I liked Virginia City, though.

I was still gambling, losing all my money at the Saw-Dust saloon each payday. I was always broke between times. A man by the name of Johnson ran the Saw-Dust, and he tried to discourage my gambling.

---

[2] *Go-devil:* This was a huge air tank with a compressed-air powered engine that would pull a string of ore cars to the main shaft, where they were hoisted to the surface.

One payday I got into a game, and as usual, I lost nearly everything I had. Suddenly, lo and behold! My luck began to change! I was playing five-card stud, and I couldn't do *anything* wrong.

Never before or since have I had such luck. I raked in the money so fast there wasn't time or room to pile it up. Much of it was in silver dollars. Nothing smaller. There were gold pieces and chips among the winnings. I could call a hand when I was beat in plain sight and still draw out on them. This upset the rest of the players so much, they complained to Johnson that I was too young to be playing in a saloon. Johnson told them he hadn't heard them complaining when they were winning all *my* money. and to keep quiet or he would shut the game down. If would have been better for me if he had; but in the long run the result would have been the same. Even the best gambler is a loser sooner or later.

ALWAYS!!

Close to morning, after I had broken many of the players, there came into the game a Chinese gentleman who was known to be one of the best gamblers in Virginia City. He had a long white beard. When Johnson saw him sit down, he worried how this would affect me. He called me over to the bar, and told me this:

"I figure you've got $1800.00. Give me $1500.00 so I can keep it for you in my safe."

This I did, and he was dead right about the amount I'd won, since I had $300.00 left. But at this point, my luck began to change.

The old Chinese man was taking my money, as well as everyone else's. I went broke sometime in the morning. Johnson had left, and wasn't due back in the saloon until later. I couldn't get any more money, so I had to give up playing.

When Johnson finally came in, I was after him immediately for the money in the safe. He refused and got mad at me. I was mad, too, crazy to be back in the game. A gambler like I was in those days doesn't think about his job, about eating or sleeping — only about gambling.

About noon I was pestering Johnson again. He wanted me to keep some of the money I had won, so he thought of a way:

"Georgie," he said, "I want you to go to the stock exchange here in town and buy a thousand dollars worth of mining stock. Then I'll give you the other $500.00 and you can go to hell with it!"

I said, "Okay." I went to the brokerage office, but it was closed. The man in charge was in the hospital with the flu.

Back I went to the saloon and told Johnson to give me the $500.00 and I would keep the thousand in his safe to buy stock with when the office re-opened.

By late afternoon I was dead broke; and again I looked up Johnson. This time he was through with me. He said nothing at all, just took all the money from the safe and handed it over. Then he said, "Goddamn you, anyway!" and walked away.

It made no impression on me, as I hurried back to the table.

I played until the next morning, when my thousand dollars was gone, and I owed the Chinaman more besides.

Dejectedly, I walked down to the mine, got what was coming to me, and paid off the Chinaman. I had about 85¢ left.

I was ashamed to face Johnson; and in fact, I never saw him again after that day.

At the mine, the foreman told me to forget the whole thing and come on back to work; but I would rather have shot myself than face anyone.

I asked the foreman to tell my boss why I wasn't coming back to work. The boss has really liked me, as I was the youngest ever to work in that mine and he liked my work.

With 85¢ in my pocket and two inches of snow on the ground, I set out for Carson City, walking down Geiger Grade in the whirling, blowing snow, and feeling sorry for myself. A man I knew came alongside with his wagon and gave me a lift. We reached Carson City after dark.

On the way I did some heavy thinking. As I saw it, I had very little choice. If I continued on my present path of destruction, gambling would be the end of me.

I made a decision then and there. It wasn't easy. I didn't gamble again for 30 years. Poker fever is hard to get rid of, but I did it!

That night I went to Van's pool hall. Van was my friend; and he gave me enough money for a room, as well as fare to Mono Lake. I paid him back soon afterward.

I didn't want to face my grandparents in Carson City, or the Burgers at Lake View.

I was ashamed of myself — no end.

 Chapter 20

"Buffalo Bill" and Other Unforgettable Basinites

After I returned to Mono Lake, I helped my grandmother for a while. I ran across some of Mono's most unusual and unforgettable characters during this time.[1] One of them was Jim Penders, who became my partner and crewmate working for the county road department.

Jim was a hard case. He was an old rounder and had prospected in most of the western mining camps at one time or another. He told me many unforgettable stories.

---

[1] Some of them may be read about in Ella Cain's book, *The Story of Bodie.*

Jim's arm was badly crippled. As a youth, while prospecting in the Mother Lode country, his burro had run off. He searched for it until dark, when he had the misfortune to fall off a steep cliff.

He ended up with an arm broken above the elbow and numerous body injuries.

Somehow, Jim had managed to get back to his camp; but it was some time before he could go for help. When he finally saw a doctor, too much time had elapsed, and the arm bones had already mended; well apart from each other. The doctor couldn't fix it. (Nowadays, of course, it would probably have been rebroken and reset.)

As part of our duties, Jim and I had to clean out the ditch south of Mono Lake.

One day after lunch, as we were sitting on the ditch bank, with Jim reading the Nevada paper he always brought along, he exclaimed, "I sure wish I had money invested in the Comstock Mine in Virginia City."

I perked right up. This was the mine I had been working in a few months earlier. The stock, he read, had gone way up.

I told Jim about the time in Virginia City when I had almost bought that same stock, before I gave it all to the Chinaman in my last game of stud poker at Johnson's.

Jim threw a fit; but I took it all pretty well. At this time I still had the philosophy, "Easy come, easy go." And *go* it usually did.

Jim had a two-story home about 200 yards south of Mono Inn, to the right of the highway about a hundred yards. In the winter of 1919, a snowslide tore down the canyon above his home one night. It demolished the house into small splinters of wood. And it took the life of my old friend Jim Penders. He is buried at the Mono Lake cemetery.

Another oddball was Mono's "Buffalo Bill," as he was called, who first came into Mono County around 1912. His real name was William Gross, and he was born on the Isle of Man.

He was well educated, but he chose to survive off the land. He topped out over six feet and was very rugged looking. His eyes were gray, almost colorless; and when he looked straight at you with his piercing gaze it was hard to forget them. He had a short white beard, and his white hair fell down over his shoulders.

Buffalo Bill wore a heavy leather jacket and a hat with a large brim. A small revolver was always in place in a holster under his left arm, as was a large knife in a sheath on his right hip. He was an impressive sight. Unlike most prospectors, he carried a huge pack on his back. In it were many different cooking utensils and supplies, rolled inside his blankets.

On the outside of the pack were his pick and shovel, and a single-shot .22 rifle. Two huge straps, crossing his back and passing over his shoulders, were buckled in front to hold the heavy pack in place.

Bill used to stop at Hammond's for provisions when Jim and I were working for the county. But actually, the first time I encountered him was about 1914. I was duck hunting at the Fisher ranch[2] with my Uncle George, when I saw a striking-looking man step out of a large hollow in a big tufa boulder. It was Buffalo Bill.

A great spring of water ran under the boulder, and an abundance of tasty watercress grew in the resulting ditch. We old-timers used to make a delicious salad out of the watercress; dressing it with vinegar and oil and a little onion. Wild ducks loved the cress and gathered there. (The ducks, though, took their cress straight, without vinegar and oil.)

Inside the tufa boulder from which Buffalo Bill emerged that day, ledges had been mortised out to make shelves for pots and pans. A natural hole at the top of the rock permitted smoke to escape. Many down-and-out people throughout the years have called this same rock home.

Uncle George and I knew the man who owned the land where the boulder sat. (It was later sold to the City of Los Angeles.)

The man's name was Caesar Civrage. He was one of Mono Basin's first settlers, arriving in 1877. He raised goats and hunting dogs, training the dogs to fetch ducks on the lake. Hunters rented them for $1.00 a day, though most hunters couldn't afford this, preferring to strip and swim into the frigid waters themselves to retrieve their ducks.

Mr. Fisher, who owned the ranch where I'd go duck hunting with Uncle George, was very intelligent and read many books in French and English.

One day, he received an urgent message from relatives in Canada pleading with him to send money so his sister could leave the country. People were extremely superstitious in those days, and she was feared to be a "witch," because she tried to communicate with the dead. Furthermore, they planned to "burn her at the stake."

Alarmed, Fisher responded immediately; and before long his sister joined him on Mono's shores.

She continued with her "seances" for local folks; and out of curiosity, George Joos and I rode down to Fisher's for a "reading." His sister sat in a dark room, in dim candlelight, for about two hours while we waited. She came out weeping, saying she had not been able to get any "vibes."

---

[2] This area is now called Danburg Beach.

George and I had been hoping for a prediction of fame and fortune. We were extremely disappointed and planned to try again another time; but we never did.

Fisher had about 300 goats. He began noticing that some of the kids were missing. A band of about 300 Paiutes lived at the crest of the hill (near Black Point). One day, as he walked through the brush, he saw some small goat skins hanging outside the wikiups. He decided then and there to ferry his goats, or a good part of the herd, to Paoha Island, where they would be safe from poachers and have ample grass and fresh water.

These were some of the same goats John Bellie and I hunted on that cold winter day, years later.

Fisher gave us some insight into Buffalo Bill's way of life: he had never been seen riding in a wagon with anyone; nor had he ever been in a saloon or cafe; he never ate at anyone's camp, nor did he invite anyone to eat at his; most of his cooking was done in the open, and roast rabbit was his main dish. Home for Buffalo Bill was a few boards and some sagebrush. Conversation with Bill was normal enough, but it was never lengthy. Like all prospectors, he always expected to find a pot of gold at the end of the rainbow. He sold some claims in Bodie and made a little stake from the sale. From time to time he'd show up at Jack Hammond's grocery store to buy slabs of bacon, beans, and baking powder, along with shells for his rifle. When next seen, he might be on the highest peak of the Sierra Nevada mountains. He fished at Mill Creek and did a lot of rabbit hunting. Like most of us, he gathered Indian tea.

Buffalo Bill had found a prospect at Ellery Lake, near the top of Tioga Pass. His diggings were about halfway up the lake on the right-hand side, where he had dug a shaft many feet deep. Whenever people asked what he'd found, or what he was looking for, Bill never answered, just pierced the questioner with that pale gray gaze of his. When he was run out of Ellery Lake country by snow, he settled in a two-story abandoned stagecoach stop at lower Wilson Creek. It was located in a dry wash, about a third of a mile beyond the Mono Lake cemetery. In fact, some remnants, boards, and "Bouncing Betty"[4] plants still mark the spot.

We locals who hunted rabbits around Buffalo Bill's house would smell the pungent aroma of rabbits roasting; but we were never invited in. It seemed like he simply did not want to have social contact with people. Some people went so far as to call him "the wolf."

For months at a time no one would see Bill; but one winter he arrived for a short stay in Bodie, while he traded small pouches of gold for

---

[3] Bouncing Betty is an exceptionally hardy, colored orchid perennial of the phlox family.

provisions at Cain's store. He intended to return to Mono Lake. Instead, he found himself snowbound in one of Bodie's famous snows: seven feet of the white stuff, and Bill without snowshoes to get out.

Bill patched up an abandoned cabin and prepared to spend some time. A miner gave him a stove that was about worn out, and others gave him a few sticks of wood. That was one of the worst winters Bodie had ever known. Blizzards kept piling snow on Bill's shack, and the few sticks of wood were quickly used up.

Now, the one thing that Bodie didn't have was wood — and you can't burn gold to keep warm. It was always nip-and-tuck for families to stay alive with what little wood they could find to store up for the winters. There was no way to import wood, or anything else, once winter had set in. So, while beans and bacon could fuel his stomach for a while, Buffalo Bill could not exist without some warmth. He started picking up a piece of wood here and there from neighbors' piles at night. Going outside with candle or lamp in hand to check out a noise, people would see Bill raiding their woodpile. When dogs barked up a storm in the night, husband would say to wife, or vice versa: "Must be Buffalo Bill stealing some more wood." But a time came, and soon, when the loss of wood ceased to be amusing.

Bill didn't hit the same woodpile every night. He reasoned that by going farther from his cabin to raid a woodpile, there'd be less of a chance that the wood would be missed. One moonlit night, as he was picking up his sticks from a neighbors' pile quite far from his own cabin, the neighbors' husky young son came out to see what the dogs were barking about. Bill tried to run, but he fell in the deep snow and the young fellow caught up with him. Understanding the predicament that the old man was in, the young fellow told him: "For this one time I'll let you keep the wood, but don't you ever come back to our house again."

Bill's closest neighbor had a wife and five kids, and their woodpile was very low. Bill had never taken much wood from them. But after another huge storm hit Bodie, Bill wasn't able to travel far for his wood, and he began stealing it from them. Now people *really* began talking about how to stop Bill from taking wood which they so desperately needed to get their families through the winter. This particular neighbor's wife put up such a fuss that her husband said he would have a talk with the old man. He found Bill in his cabin, warm and solid as an old oak tree. It was evident that the desperate winter had not dampened Bill's spirits.

"Bill," said his neighbor, "we've been looking at our woodpile, my wife and I, and we know it's going to be nip-and-tuck to make it through the winter with our small amount of wood. If you keep taking it, we'll all freeze. I don't want you to come after our wood again, Bill, or there's going to be trouble."

All he got out of Bill was a grunt; but he went back and told his wife that he'd had a long talk with him and had scared him off. Shortly after this, yet another blizzard hit. Tracks in the snow showed his neighbor's wife that Bill was again making nighttime visits to the woodpile.

Knowing it was no use reasoning with Bill, the neighbor talked it over with his buddy at the mine. This was a big Italian miner, and he was pretty mad himself about Bill's raids on his own woodpile. He summed up the situation like this: "You have two choices. You can shoot him and kill him. Or, you can figure out some way to scare the hell out of him. I know a way, but it's dangerous and you may not want to go for it. Still, it might save your woodpile."

The neighbor said, "Outside of murder, I'll try anything."

The Italian outlined his plan. Get a round piece of wood and gouge out the center. Take a quarter of a stick of dynamite and a cap, put it in the center of the wood and nail the hollow shut. Then lay it on the woodpile where Bill couldn't miss it. Bill's neighbor decided to proceed.

The trap was ready. However, three nights passed without that particular piece being picked up. Bill was still stealing their wood, but that stick stayed put. His neighbor was puzzled no end.

At about four o'clock on the morning of the fourth night, snowbound Bodie was the scene of a terrific explosion. People ran through the snowdrifts with candles and lanterns to see what in the world had happened. Most of Bodie found themselves gathered around Buffalo Bill's cabin. Or what used to be a cabin: the roof was blown off; the walls were caved in, and the little stove had been blown to pieces and scattered in the snow.

Bill fled hastily into the night, clad only in somewhat singed long-johns. Known as a man of few words, that night Bill smashed his reputation to smithereens. He kept shouting over and over: "Somebody has blown my cabin up! Somebody has blown my cabin up!" Strangely enough, the little chair and table at which he sat and ate were standing intact in the middle of the floor, untouched by the force of the explosion.

Bill was so pathetic, running around in the snow trying to locate his belongings, that his neighbors forget his thievery and pitched in to help him. They found his rifle, pots and pans, and a few other things. One neighbor took him in for the night to keep him from freezing, and later, there was a town meeting to decide what to do about the old fellow. The man at the livery stable offered to let him stay there until spring. Bill helped with the chores to pay for his keep.

When spring came, Buffalo Bill got his pack together and returned to the old stagecoach house at Wilson Creek. That summer he prospected in the mountains same as ever, evidently no worse off for his explosive winter in Bodie.

Tall and lanky Tom Lawrence was a personal friend of mine. He was a school teacher from Chicago, who came to Mono County to search for gold. Many of us heard him quote Shakespeare and speak Latin. He was born in 1879. His headquarters was Bridgeport, but he worked high in the hills of Masonic at the Chaung Mine. He was a hard core miner — they were called "Boomers," or "ten-day men." On February 12, 1938, Tom left Masonic on foot in a raging blizzard, headed for Bridgeport. Somehow, he got off course, wandering over to the left. Near the Point Ranch, he took shelter in a bunch of willows, trampling snow and breaking off branches in an attempt to keep his hands from freezing.

A search party found him much later, frozen to death. Most of us Basinites know his beautiful — and prophetic — poem, originally titled "Meditation," but called most often "Mono in the Springtime."

Mono gulls.

Mono in the Springtime

How soon will Mono's fountains
    smash the web winter has spun,
And Mighty Mono's mountains flash
    their welcome to the sun?
I count each day the tortured hours
    and try to hide the sting
Til nature's breath awakes the flowers
When Mono smiles in Spring.

When cold, depressing winter haunts
    my thoughts with stories weird,
And want's grim, silent shadow
    haunts me 'til my soul grows tired.
When storm withers flowers and
    tree and streams no longer sing,
I try to fancy how 'twill be
When Mono smiles in spring.

The mountains fill with icy shot
    the bitter, piercing wind,
Yet in their wildest wrath they're
    not than man himself less kind;
Though they be merciless as death,
    when Winter rules as king,
They soothe you with a perfumed breath
When Mono smiles in Spring.

I seek not for a useless tear that
    any man may shed;
I seek not for a careless prayer,
    when I have joined the dead.
I seek not for the why and where
    of mad imagining,
But I would like to wake each year
When Mono smiles in Spring.

Tom Lawrence

Chapter 21

The Love Bug and I

I've already mentioned some of my adventures while employed by the Sierra Power Company as a patrolman. My cousin Lester Filosena and I took a job with the same power company in the summer of 1920, as caretakers at Gem Lake.

This lake is at an elevation of 10,000 feet in the Minaret wilderness. You reach it by a steep, primitive tramway, or by a narrow trail, suitable only for foot or horseback. This trail originated at the Silver Lake[1] power plant.

Our job was to control the flow of water through the dams located at Gem and Agnew Lakes. These dams collected run-off water from other lakes and streams in the high country, such as Garnet, Ediza, Thousand Islands, and Waugh. We regulated the valves controlling the amount of water to the power plant below, where it was used to generate electricity for Mono Basin.

We kept the electric lines up, and the telephone line in operation. I reported weather conditions and the current water level at 9:00 a.m. daily, when I'd receive our orders for the day.

In the late fall, Lester and two others who had been working there resigned. They didn't want to be isolated during the long winter months, where the only mode of travel out in winter was by way of snowshoes.

Mr. Watts, my boss, told me that if I would stay, I could hire a friend. I knew just the person: Sky Arribalsage. He was a Spaniard who was living at Jack Hammond's place. Sky asked about the job and its duties.

"Doing nothing, mostly," I said, "just keeping me company."

"I've been looking for a job like that all my life. I'll take it!" he said. "When do I start?"

I said, "Today!"

With that settled, Sky and I started out for Gem Lake.

After some time at the lake, we became bored with so little to do; so we set out a trap line and during the winter we trapped 20 marten and a fox. I was anxious to save up a little grub stake, as I hoped to go to Oklahoma in the spring to see J.B. again.

The winter was uneventful; and in the spring Sky returned to Hammond's, while I took the train out of Carson City to El Reno. J.B. was waiting for me.

In El Reno I found work after a few days on the line crew for the telephone company. I became friendly with a young crew member who soon left for Alaska. Before he did, he gave me the address of a girl named Betty (Elizabeth) Oakwood, whom he had met while in Tyrone, Pennsylvania. She had some young brothers and sisters and a dog named Rags. I've always had a soft spot for dogs, you know, and I began writing to Betty. She liked my letters and I liked hers. We exchanged pictures, and I could see she looked like a winner. I decided to go to Pennsylvania to meet her.

Betty was as pretty as her picture. Prettier, in fact! So I stayed. In

Betty and "Rags."

Newlyweds, Betty and George, in Jenette, Pennsylvania, 1922.

Tyrone I got a job on the telephone crew, and we would meet while I was out working. The love bug had bitten me — HARD!

The only drawback was her parents. They had not met many westerners, did not know my family background or my intentions; and they refused to let us establish any kind of relationship. (That's why we met while I worked.) Naturally, this made us all the more determined to see each other. One of her relatives was affiliated with the "Klan," and I heard rumors that I might be escorted out of town — forcibly. I didn't relish the prospect, so I went back to El Reno to let things cool off. I visited with J.B. and waited for word from Betty.

I was on cloud nine when I finally got a letter from her saying, "Come back and we'll talk things over." I told my father I was going to get married if things could be worked out. He loaned me $400.00, gave me his blessings and waved lovesick me off. Once more, I headed for Pennsylvania.

I was sorry to learn that Betty's parents hadn't changed their mind about our relationship. There was no other course but to take matters into our own hands, so to speak.

Betty's parents thought that we might elope in the middle of the night. I surprised them and whisked her away at high noon!! Nobody saw us!!

The date was Saturday, May 27, 1922. The old taxi driver who picked us up in Tyrone told us we would have to travel fast, as we had to cross the border into Cumberland, Maryland, where the courthouse was only open until one. Betty was only 17, which was the legal age in Maryland, but not in Pennsylvania.

We got our license, then stopped at a jeweler's where I bought Betty a gold wedding ring. From there it was on to the Methodist church, where a crippled old minister married us. His wife, Ada, was our witness. Their name, I remember, was Childress.

The taxi driver took us to his own home, where he rented out rooms. We stayed there two days while we looked for an apartment.

Our wedding supper, at a small restaurant, was ham and sweet potatoes (still one of our favorites); and we were in high spirits.

We found a tiny "love nest," and every day I looked in vain for work. Ten days passed, and our money ran pretty low. Betty said, "Let's go home. Maybe things will be better now."

At Tyrone, we rode the street car out to the Oakwood's house on the hill. Betty's mother, Bess, came to the door. Her husband, Frank, whose word was law, had left strict orders that I should never set foot inside their door. Bess reluctantly turned me away, permitting Betty to remain and visit. Before I returned to town, I told Betty to come to the Arlington Towers Hotel when she was ready to go home.

It was very late in the evening and I was very nervous. I was greatly relieved when I finally saw my bride at the door.

We spent the night there, returning to Cumberland the next day, disappointed that there was nothing for us in Tyrone.

Our financial situation became desperate. I remembered that my friend Sky had told me to write him if I ever needed anything. I figured this was the time, so I wrote, asking for $160.00 to tide us over.

In the meantime, a large woman named Kate agreed to give us $30 to $40 credit at her grocery store. Betty and I enjoyed shopping for "White Goose" coffee and other staples.

At one point, we didn't even have enough money for a postage stamp, and we were literally "living on love."

I haunted the post office for the check from Sky, and were we ever upset when we finally went to the bank to cash it. They had lost it!

I had to write Sky to issue a new one; and by now Betty and I were *really* in a pickle! We owed money for rent, as well as groceries.

One morning, before I was out of bed, there was a knock at the door, and a man called out, "Is your name George La Braque?"

I answered, "Yes," and let the man in.

He said, "We have a job for you as a laborer where you registered for work at the Kelly Springfield Tire Company. The wages are 30¢ per hour, 12 hours a day, 15 minutes for lunch. Want to take it?"

"You bet!!" I answered. I reported for work the next morning. After learning the trade, I stepped up to doing "piece work," at which time I made six or seven dollars a day.

The working conditions were unbearable. I got run down and sick from the long hours and back-breaking work. Betty's newly married cousin, Liz Deome, and her husband Fred came to visit us. They talked us into moving in with them and their parents in the neighboring town of Irwin. Fred helped me get a job at the Vacuum Tire Company making tires. Soon we were able to move into a place of our own. It had a huge grapevine on one side. This was not a bit too soon, as we now had a baby on the way.

Two months before the baby was due, Betty woke me at daylight, insisting the baby was coming. She told me to call Dr. Smith, her doctor, right away.

Dr. Smith was eating breakfast, and seemed vague as to who we were. Nevertheless, I hurriedly gave him directions, and he said he would be right over. I flew upstairs and told the landlady that Betty needed help while I phoned to tell my boss that I would not be in to work.

When I returned to the house, I was stunned to find that the landlady, who happened to be a midwife, had helped Betty deliver a five-pound baby girl. We named her Lily.

When Dr. Smith arrived soon afterward, I saw why he hadn't known us: he was an entirely different Dr. Smith! Nevertheless, he looked things over and pronounced mother and baby doing "fine." Then he returned to his meal.

We had planned to buy baby clothes on the next payday; so Lily had literally "not a stitch to wear." Betty handed me our last two dollars, and instructed me to buy some baby clothes — pronto! I rushed to the nearest store and made a purchase. I arrived home, breathless but proud, and handed Betty a long, lacy Christening dress — nothing more! Betty sure was upset. Lily, however, did fine, wrapped in petticoats and tucked into a shoebox bed.

A year or two later, we moved to a house in Jeanette, down on the river bank. It was owned by an old Polish couple who kept ducks and chickens. No children were allowed there; but after Lily climbed onto the husband's lap, we were allowed to stay.

My daughter Lily, age 4 years.

One rainy Sunday, I said to Betty, "Let's go to the auction today." This we did, and while there I bought a gold watch. It had rained hard all day, and that evening, as we undressed by the fireplace, we noticed water pouring in under the door. Alarmed, I said, "I wonder what the hell is going on?"

I was shocked as I realized it was a flood. Even worse, our house was at the river's edge. I shouted, "Gather up a few things, while I get the chickens (we had 14 of our own), and we'll get the heck out.

"The heck with the chickens," Betty argued.

"No sir," I insisted, "I'm going to save those chickens."

Outside, I grabbed the chickens by the legs and threw them inside the house, where they immediately flew upstairs. By the time we left the house, the water was up to my waist. My heart was in my throat as I clutched my wife and baby tightly to my chest, wading in terror through the raging waters toward higher ground. There we found many other fleeing families.

We were shivering and soaking wet, as we made our way to the train station to find shelter. Others had had the same idea; and it was so crowded that we couldn't even sit down. In desperation, I said to Betty, "Let's get on a train and go somewhere." I went to the ticket agent and asked when the next train was due.

He asked, "Where to?"

"I don't give a hoot!" I replied. "Just so we get out of here." We boarded the next train and rode to the end of the line. Then we got off and caught the next train back.

It was dawn when we arrived back in Jeanette. Some good news and some bad news were waiting for us.

The river had subsided, but we faced a terrible job of cleaning up six inches of mud and silt on the floor of our house. In despair, Betty pleaded with me to move; but our finances would not allow this, so the mop-up began.

The only thing to crow about was the chicken situation. They had roosted on the curtain rods and the piano, and not one had been lost.

During the next three years (1924-27) we saved enough money to buy a used Model T. Soon afterward, unfortunately, a stike at the tire plant left me unemployed. The Great Depression was shaping up, and jobs were very scarce.

As our money cup ran low, I was lucky to find work at a nearby glass factory hauling glass to the cutter's with an electric cart.

Conditions at the plant were bad, as usual, but I was shocked to see how badly the Negroes were treated. The work was very hard, and there

"California, Here I Come"—in my Model T, 1927.

were huge rats to deal with. One night, as I was eating my supper, a gigantic rat tried to steal my food. It bit me on the leg when I did not cooperate.

This was too much for me. I said to Betty, "We are going to California! Back to Mono Lake!"

The idea of returning to Mono Lake had been brewing in my mind. Only a few days earlier, the Sierra Power Company had sent me a telegram offering me a job as an operator at the Silver Lake plant. The salary was $125.00 per month, plus housing and utilities, too good an offer to pass up.

It was 1927. Betty was reluctant to leave her family; but I was determined to take the job.

In preparation, we sold our furniture, packed our belongings, and made some adjustments on the Model T. As for the chickens, they didn't fare as well this time, ending up in our stew pot.

In May, with spirits high, we headed back to Mono Basin.

At that time, except for one small stretch, there were no paved roads. When it rained for any length of time, the roads were deep ruts of solid mud. Impassable.

In Iowa we stopped to camp one evening and Lily, now four, reached out to pet a dog. It bit her clear through the skin above the eyebrow, and

My uncle, George Filosena, with my son, George, Jr., 1936.

J.B. and granddaughter Lily, at the Filosena ranch.

My wife, Betty, at Rush Creek Power Plant.

she still has the scar. The blood flowed heavily, and Betty and I were very upset. A little old lady doctored her with mercurochrome, considered a cure-all in those days.

As luck would have it, because of the heavy rain we were stranded there for nine days, with only boiled potatoes and a little salt to eat. Finally, the sun came out and the mud dried up.

We resumed our journey, stopping next at the "Great Salt Lake." We rested there, swimming and floating in the briny waters.

It took us 21 days to reach Mono Basin. We stopped at Conway Summit, treating ourselves to hot apple pie at the roadside inn. (Although over 50 years have passed, their hot apple pie is still a favorite of mine.)

As we slowly made our way downward through the steep, hairpin curves, Betty got her first view of Mono Lake, with its islands and picturesque craters. She was enchanted to find her new home so beautiful.

About an hour later, we drove up to the Filosena ranch in a cloud of dust. I proudly introduced Grandmother Mary and Uncle George to my family.

My homecoming was marred by the news of George Joos' death the previous winter, as he tended his trap line near Gem Lake.

We moved into a house high on a hill at the Silver Lake plant, and I went to work as an oiler. We became good friends with the Carsons of Carson Camp. Betty and Lily often walked down the road to have tea there.

One day, when Betty and Lily returned from visiting the Carsons, they insisted it had rained small frogs; and indeed, Lily had some in a tin can. I still remain dubious, although I have heard of this phenomenon.

Later, we transferred to Mill Creek, only a mile and a half walk to the Filosena ranch (by footpath over the hill). Lily, who was five, was enrolled at the Mono Lake School (now the Keller residence).

That same winter Betty suffered a miscarriage. Her life was saved when Dr. Kelly of Bridgeport skied in several miles during a heavy blizzard to give her professional attention.

We moved to the Lee Vining Power plant, where two more children were born: a son, George, Jr., in January 1932, and another daughter, Donna Elizabeth, in 1937.

Uncle George came to live with us when the Filosena ranch was sold to the City of Los Angeles. He passed away in 1934.

If the truth were to be told, the conditions that prevailed during the winter of 1931-32, when my son was born, played a big part in changing the lives of Mono Basin inhabitants.

Chapter 22

Snow Baby

One evening in the fall of 1931, an urgent meeting was held at the Mono Lake schoolhouse. We residents hoped to force the California legislature to provide funding for a snow removal program that would facilitate year-round travel.

Meetings on this subject had been held many times before, without results. The answer from the State was always the same! No money to be allocated for snow removal in Mono County.

Our County Supervisor, Venita McPherson,[1] had been pushing hard for a similar program. For years she had pleaded with the other supervisors from outlying districts for their support, but she was always met with a cold shoulder and disinterest.

Help came from an unexpected source when "Mother Nature" intervened. Several feet of snow fell early in the winter of 1931; then, on Christmas day, an intense storm began, raging for several days. It blocked the already impassable roads with huge mountains of snow.

This new snow, resting on top of the hardened snow crust, caused slides north and south. There was no possible way for residents to get out, except for skis, snowshoes, toboggans, or by hiring Tex Cushion and his dog sleds from Mammoth Lakes. Tex had a government contract for mail delivery during the winter months. He also hauled provisions, and could be hired for short, pleasure rides or for a long haul.

We were one of many families who were inconvenienced, and even threatened, by the lack of an open road. Betty, for example, was in her final months of pregnancy. Others were very ill and in need of medical attention.

Supervisor McPherson called Governor Rolph in Sacramento, telling him of Betty's predicament and other emergencies, and asking for his help. Her persuasion and pleading finally got to him. The Governor agreed to take immediate action. If Mono residents could dig through

---

[1] Venita was also owner and proprietor of Mono Inn from 1921-1958.

Tex Cushion's dog sled at Casa Diablo, near Mammoth, California. The geyser has been capped.

Tex Cushion's dog team (George Allison, driver), with LaBraque family on sled. Main St., Lee Vining, 1936.

from their side, snow removal equipment would come to meet them from the other side.

At an emergency meeting the townspeople settled on a route over McPherson grade to the east, the snow there being not quite so deep as by the southern route through Dead Man. The route chosen would take them 45 miles east to Benton, then 25 miles south to Bishop.

The men would shovel their way out. Many able-bodied men volunteered to help. The going was slow. It took us three days to reach Rush Creek. A heavy Mono fog had come in after the storm, hampering visibility and chilling us to the bone. At these times a heavy "pogonip," or frost, coats the landscape, and the sun never comes out.

I had a personal reason for shoveling as hard as I did. A caravan of 15 cars was being formed in Lee Vining, to the south. I would have Betty on it. She would then be able to go to the Bohn Maternity home in Bishop to await our child in safety. I realized it was still early in the winter, and that we would most likely be snowbound again before long.

Some of the men who shoveled with me were Guy Carrington, Gus and Bill Hess, Charlie Adair, Clay Calhoun, Bill Donnelly and Howard McAfee, as well as Power Company workers and many Indian men.

It was our tenth day of shoveling. Our backs were aching, our hands blistered, and we were exhausted. Suddenly, we heard the faint rumble of machinery. The plows broke through to meet us just at dark, January 7, 1932, just this side of McPherson grade. As they approached we threw down our shovels. We cheered and waved our arms.

Betty and I were apprehensive when she got into the car that would take her and Alice Montrose, a student, to Bishop. Although we were reluctant to be separated (I would have to work and care for ten-year-old Lily), we recalled Betty's earlier miscarriage and didn't want to take any chances.

The road was barely passable after the shoveling, and a Caterpillar pulled the car carrying Betty over the deep ruts. Sure enough, the rough jolting caused Betty to go into labor early.

In the same caravan were two Dodge trucks driven by Bill and Gus Hess. They were to return with groceries and supplies for those who were snowbound. Dairy products were still available to us, for Pearl Mattly, who had a dairy two miles south of Lee Vining, made deliveries with horse-drawn sleds equipped with steel runners.

Bill Banta, a local peddler, brought in a load of fresh produce. Katy Adair,[2] who was living at the Cain ranch that winter, remembers how

---

[2] Now Katy (Conway) Bell.

glad she was to see the many car headlights coming from Benton road that night. They received a crate of oranges, and they sat on the floor eating them until the juice ran down their arms.

We had no telephones in our homes at this time, so I did not know the ordeal Betty was going through that night.

In the morning I was awakened by a call on the Power Company telephone, with a message that I had a son. The news was dampened by the fact that our premature baby was in critical condition. Several anxious days were spent until I received word that he was out of danger. Fortunately, Betty made a speedy recovery.

A few days later, with the hardships forgotten, Uncle George and I went to Bishop to see my new son. We named him George Rolph Dewey La Braque. He was born January 8, 1932.

Uncle George and I left at daylight, by way of McPherson Grade via Warm Springs, returning just as a storm was coming in. We were in our Chevy, and we had one heck of a rough trip. The roads closed right behind us, and it was a full six weeks before Betty and the baby could come home.

Governor Rolph had kept a close watch on the rescue attempt and the snow removal operation. Reporters wrote accounts of our "snow baby," and gave a detailed account of the plight Basinites had been in.

Governor Rolph sent a telegram, congratulating the La Braque family on the birth of their son.

In June of the following summer, Governor Rolph arrived in the Basin in a chauffeur-driven limousine, his entourage following him in another. Both cars had small American flags mounted on the fenders. He came to our home to have pictures taken with the "snow baby" and his parents.

Open Roads

Everyone had high praise for Venita McPherson, but she wasn't one to rest on her laurels. One of her pet projects was to get a paved road from Hawthorne, Nevada, to Mono Basin. This would connect California and Nevada, and meet up with Highway 395.

Many years of rough going by wagon trail and dirt road marked the history of this route.

After ten years of persistent effort, Venita, who was supported by a strong lobby from Charlie Hendel, the Assemblyman from Hawthorne,

1933: Betty, with Governor Rolph holding George, Jr.

18VZ W 38 DL

> SACRAMENTO CALIF
> 1053A JAN 9 1932

MRS GEORGE LA BRAQUE
> BISHOP CALIF

I CONGRATULATE YOU UPON THE BIRTH OF YOUR SON YESTERDAY STOP THE WHOLE STATE HAS BEEN INTERESTED IN YOU AND NOW REJOICE IN YOUR MOTHERHOOD YOUR SON AND THE PROUD AND HAPPY FATHER OF THE FAMILY VERY SINCERELY

> JAMES ROLPH JR
> GOVERNOR OF CALIFORNIA
> 1718A

Nevada, saw Route 167 started in June 1948, with much of the work done by the Isabell Construction Company.

It was completed in sections, and was dedicated at the State line on October 17, 1957. It is commonly called the "Pole Line" road, as it closely follows the telephone lines. Unlike other roads in the County, the "Pole Line" road had no snow removal problem to speak of.

(L:) Wallis and Venita McPherson with son, Wallis, Jr. (R:) Venita at piano.

Dedication of Pole Line Rd. (Rte 167), 1957. Supervisor McPherson is fourth from left.

Until 1932, snow removal — or what there was of it — was accomplished either by a dump truck with a blade, or by a caterpillar tractor pulling a motorless grader or equipped with a wooden blade.

After the harsh winter of 1932, Governor Rolph was convinced that snow removal for Mono County was definitely a "must." With this in mind, he ordered State engineers to come up with a vehicle specifically designed for this purpose.

One fellow recalled how trains like the "Slim Princess" kept their tracks open with the use of a catcher, a large railroad fan mounted on the front of the engines.

With this in mind,[3] a five-ton truck chassis was equipped with a railroad-type rotary. The business end of it suggested a gargantuan demon with bat ears and a great, gaping maw, full of whirling steel blades for teeth. The rotary motor was powered by a Liberty aviation engine. This unlikely looking rig operated at a speed of three miles an hour. It was called a "Snow-Go," and newer models retain the name.

The "Go" left Bishop in January 1933, taking Highway 395 North. It took 45 days to reach June Lake Junction, a distance of 55 miles.

Because of its strange peculiarities, the only time it was on the road was when it was crossing it, so to speak. It steered from both ends, and the controls were backwards, so a "swamper" relayed directions to the driver, who navigated by the seat of his pants. When the snow was blowing, which was often, the fan threw the snow high in the air behind the "Go," blocking the road and no-one could follow.

Evidently accuracy was not one of its attributes: a picture of the "Go," sitting a hundred yards from the road, was taken in the spring. This picture was mounted in the Departmental Office in Bishop, with the caption, "What the heck is it doing here?"

Improvements were definitely called for in the "Go's" design. The following winter a new, improved version came into operation, and Mono was open to year-round traffic.

When the first "Go" came into sight, it was a sunny day, with sparkling blue skies. Betty, Lily, and I watched in awe as the "Go" threw the snow high in a feathery arc. It was like a fairy tale come true.

High Hopes

Like Christian Mattly, I had a hunch the town of Lee Vining would prosper. With some financial help from a dubious J.B. (he always referred to Lee Vining as "Poverty Flat"), I bought several lots in the town proper.

---

[3] California Highway and Public Works, September 1933.

1. Tractor pulling motorless grader near "Smoky Bear Flat."
2. First "Sno-Go," 1932. Foreman Norman Van Dyke and dog, Crestview, California.
3. Experimental model of a "Sno-Go."
4. Auger-type snow plow in common use today.

My uncle Frank Donnelly (who had married little Mary Filosena) taught me the fundamentals of carpentry; and in 1936, I built a large, sturdy home at Fourth Street (where Betty and I live today). Later, I built a sixteen-unit motel and a gas station. Even though I had only a fourth-grade education I was able to do my own plumbing and electrical work.

In the evenings, Betty coached me with my spelling and math; and I learned to speak Spanish fluently.

In 1940, when World War II began, we moved to Vallejo, California, where I went to work in the Mare Island Navy Yard, operating one of their eleven D.C. power plants that supplied power to ships under construction or in need of repair.

As a national emergency existed, I could not be cleared for work unless I held a valid birth certificate. I got this by obtaining affidavits from Nellie Reynolds, who had worked for my Grandmother Mary, and Mrs. Jake Mattly, the midwife who had delivered me.

After the war I felt Mono calling; so we returned to Mono Basin to operate the La Braque Motel.

Lily married Pete Mathieu, a son of August and Marie Mathieu, French immigrants and early Mono County settlers of Benton, California. She is widowed, and lives near us in Lee Vining. My son, George, married

My daughter Donna Erneta on the Lockhart Ranch in Barstow.

an English lass named Wendy Jackson. They own and operate the Ojai Indian Shop in Ojai, California. Our youngest daughter, Donna, surprised us by carrying on the old family tradition of "sheep-raising." She and her husband, Pedro Erneta, a native of Spain, are in partnership with Louis Curucchet. They operate the Mono Sheep Company.

I have seen many changes over the years, and I am particularly concerned about the receding shoreline of Mono Lake. This didn't happen overnight, but began innocently enough around 1930, Basinites (including the Filosenas) sold the largest part of their water rights to the City of Los Angeles. We thought there was enough water for all. How wrong we all were!!

The next step was the construction of a large tunnel at East Portal, near the base of the Mono Craters, which diverted a large part of Mono Basin water southward. The water was taken from tributaries which, up to now, have fed the lake.

By 1975, Mono Lake had dropped over 40 feet. It seemed that the lake was doomed until a small group of ornithologists, led by David and Sally Gaines, started a campaign to "Save Mono Lake." The most devastating event we witnessed, was when Negit Island, the nesting place of the largest percentage of California gulls, became a peninsula. This left the gull eggs and chicks defenseless against coyotes and rodents.

Through the efforts of the Mono Lake Committee, steps are being taken to make Mono and its surrounding shores a national monument, and hopes are high that Mono will be preserved and protected for future generations to enjoy.

Yes, Mono has been good to me. We have seven grandchildren and three great-grandchildren. Betty and I celebrated our sixty-second anniversary in May 1984.

I was awakened this morning by the faint cries of the ever-returning gulls, mere specks against the sky. They were back once more to share Mono in the Springtime with me, the man from Mono.

Mono Lake Patriarch, George LaBraque.

An Indian Prayer

O great spirit, whose breath gives life to all the world, hear me! I am small and weak. I need your strength.

Let me walk in beauty, and make my eyes behold
the red and purple sunset.

Make my hands respect the things you have made, and my ears
sharp to hear your voice.

Make me wise so that I may understand the things
you have taught my people.

Let me learn the lessons you have hidden
in every leaf and rock.

I seek strength, not to be greater than my brother,
but to fight my greatest enemy — myself.

Make me always ready to come to you with clean hands
and straight eyes.

So when life fades, as the fading sunset,
my spirit may come to you without shame.

Author unknown